Celebrate
THE Century®

A COLLECTION OF
COMMEMORATIVE STAMPS

1970-1979

UNITED STATES POSTAL SERVICE

POSTMASTER GENERAL
AND CHIEF EXECUTIVE OFFICER
William J. Henderson

SENIOR VICE PRESIDENT, GOVERNMENT
RELATIONS AND PUBLIC POLICY
Deborah K. Willite

VICE PRESIDENT, PUBLIC AFFAIRS
AND COMMUNICATIONS
Azeezaly S. Jaffer

MANAGER, PROMOTIONS
Gary A. Thuro Jr.

PROJECT MANAGER
Clarence R. Williams

TIME-LIFE BOOKS IS A DIVISION OF TIME LIFE INC.

TIME-LIFE TRADE PUBLISHING

VICE PRESIDENT AND PUBLISHER
Neil Levin

DIRECTOR OF NEW PRODUCT DEVELOPMENT
Teresa Graham

PROJECT COORDINATOR
Jennifer L. Ward

PRINTING PRODUCTION MANAGER
Vanessa Hunnibell

EDITORIAL STAFF FOR CELEBRATE THE CENTURY

MANAGING EDITOR
Morin Bishop

EDITORS
John Bolster, Sarah Brash

DESIGNERS
Barbara Chilenskas, Jia Baek

WRITERS/RESEARCHERS
*Ward Calhoun, Theresa Deal,
Rachael Nevins, Ylann Schemm*

PHOTO EDITOR
Bill Broyles

First printing. Printed in U.S.A.

TIME-LIFE is a trademark of Time Warner Inc., and affiliated companies.

LIBRARY OF CONGRESS CATALOGING-IN-PUBLICATION DATA
Celebrate the century: a collection of commemorative stamps.
p. cm.   Includes index.
Contents: v. 8. 1970–1979
ISBN 0-7835-5324-2
1. Commemorative postage stamps—United States—History—20th century.
2. United States—History—20th century.
I. Time-Life Books

HE6185.U5C45 1998   97–46952
769.56973—DC21   CIP

Books produced by Time-Life Trade Publishing are available at a special bulk discount for promotional and premium use. Custom adaptations can also be created to meet your specific marketing goals. Call 1-800-323-5255.

PICTURE CREDITS

Cover, J. P. Laffont/Sygma; 4, CBS Photo Archive/Archive Photos; 5, Dennis Stock/Magnum; 6, Henri Cartier Bresson/Magnum; 7, Vernon Biever; 8, Movie Still Archives; 9, Burt Glinn/Magnum; 10, Doug Wilson/Black Star; 11, Dennis Brack/Black Star; 12, top left, AP/Wide World Photos; top right, Superstock; inset, Archive Photos; 13, Dennis Brack/Black Star; 14, top left, Dennis Stock/Magnum; inset, Bernard Gotfryd/Archive Photos; 14-15, Herbert Eisenberg/Globe Photos; 15, Charles Moore/Black Star; 16, ABC/NFL Photos; 17, ABC Photos; 18, inset, ABC Photos; bottom, Tony Tomsic/NFL Photos; 19, Tony Tomsic/NFL Photos; 20, Ken Regan/Camera 5; 21, both, ABC Photos; 22, The Boeing Company; 23, The Boeing Company; 24, The Boeing Company; 25, top and bottom, The Boeing Company; 26, The Boeing Company; 27, top, The Boeing Company; bottom, United Airlines; 28, Children's Television Workshop; 29, top, Children's Television Workshop; stamp, Big Bird © The Jim Henson Company; *Sesame Street* is a trademark of the Children's Television Workshop; 30, Archive Photos; 31, all, Children's Television Workshop; 32, left, Children's Television Workshop; right, Movie Still Archives; 33, left, Children's Television Workshop; top right, Tom Caffrey/Globe Photos; bottom right, Children's Television Workshop; 34, David Falconer/Black Star; 35, Wally McNamee/Woodfin Camp; 36, David Sheffield/Woodfin Camp; 37, top, Arthur Grace/Sygma; bottom, Wally McNamee/Woodfin Camp; 38, top, Tom Ebenhoh/Black Star; bottom left, Baron Wolman/Woodfin Camp; bottom right, Doug Wilson/Black Star; 39, Gerald Holly/Black Star; 41, JVC Corp.; 42, inset, Gaslight Advertising Archives; remaining, Corbis-Bettmann; 44, Ken Regan/Camera 5; 45, top, Corbis-Bettmann; stamp, Secretariat™ Thoroughbred Owners & Breeders Association, Lexington, KY; 46, Neil Leifer/*Sports Illustrated;* 46-47, UPI/Corbis-Bettmann; 47, both, Ken Regan/Camera 5; 48, Ken Regan/Camera 5; 49, top left, Ken Regan/Camera 5; top center, Neil Leifer/*Sports Illustrated;* top right, UPI/Corbis-Bettmann; bottom, UPI/Corbis-Bettmann; 50-54, Ames Research Center/NASA; 55, TRW, Inc.; 56, Movie Still Archives; 57, top, CBS Photo Archive; stamp, "All in the Family" © CPT Holdings, Inc.; 58, top, CBS Photo Archive; inset, AP/Wide World Photos; 59, Courtesy Columbia TriStar; 60, top, Movie Still Archives; bottom, CBS Photo Archive; 61, CBS Photo Archive; 62, Neil Leifer; 63, Vernon J. Biever; 64, left, Tony Tomsic/NFL Photos; inset, Walter Iooss Jr./*Sports Illustrated;* 65, Richard Pilling/NFL Photos; 66, top, Marvin Newman/*Sports Illustrated;* inset, Walter Iooss Jr./*Sports Illustrated;* 67, Heinz Kluetmeier/*Sports Illustrated;* 68, John Olsen; 69, Flip Schulke/Corbis; 70, top left, J. P. Laffont/Sygma; inset, Peter Gould/FPG; 71, Arthur Grace/Sygma; 72, top, Christina Thomson/Woodfin Camp; bottom, Constantine Manos/Magnum; 73, Jacques C. Paucker/Globe Photos; 74, Superstock; 75, Dr. Robert S. Ledley; 76, both, Dr. Robert S. Ledley; 77, top, Kenneth Garrett/Woodfin Camp; bottom, Stock Boston; 78, top, FPG; bottom, Superstock; 79, Superstock; 80, Photo by Laura B. Kozlowski/Pozneroy Collection; 81, Tony Stone Images; 82, top left, The Arizona Republic; top right, Photo by Laura B. Kozlowski/Pozneroy Collection; inset, Michael Abramson/Black Star; 83, left, AP/Wide World Photos; inset, Harvey Ball Collection; 84, UPI/Corbis-Bettmann; 85, Ken Regan/Camera 5; 86, Black Star; 87, top, Underwood Photo Archives, SF; bottom left, Underwood Photo Archives, SF; bottom right, Hulton-Deutsch/Corbis; 88, top left, Archive Photos; top right, Leonard Freed/Magnum; bottom right, UPI/Corbis-Bettmann; 89, left, Hulton-Deutsch/Corbis; right, Tony Howarth/Woodfin Camp; 90, Movie Still Archives; 91, Corbis; 92, A. Tannenbaum/Sygma; 93, both, Waring Abbott/Michael Ochs Archives; 94-95, all, A. Tannenbaum/Sygma.

CONTENTS

Americans tuned in to *All in the Family* on **Saturday** nights (left) and inaugurated Earth Day in 1970 (above).

INTRODUCTION

The new television show that premiered on January 12, 1971, was the polarized United States in microcosm. In the Bunker family home in Queens, paterfamilias Archie and his live-in son-in-law Mike Stivic did battle on Saturday evenings from the opposite sides of a seemingly unbridgeable divide. Dyed-in-the-wool conservative and knee-jerk bigot Archie railed against peaceniks, pinkos, commies, long-haired men, short-haired women and bleeding-heart liberals, among which Mike proudly counted himself. A child of the radical '60s, he marched in peace demonstrations, admired Cuban guerrilla leader Ernesto "Che" Guevara and sported a Guevara-style mustache, casually accepted Archie's financial support as a baby boomer's due while he studied for a sociology degree, and decried the Vietnam War, racial strife, pollution and poverty.

Archie, an old-fashioned patriot, took the "love-it-or-leave-it" position: You either accepted America with all its warts or you went somewhere else. Mike wanted to get rid of the warts, now. Viewers could laugh when the two opinionated, stubborn men lobbed charges and counter-charges at each other, but the divisions in the real world of the '70s were painfully deep and bitter—in truth, nothing that laughter could relieve. What weighed most heavily on American minds at the dawn of the decade was the war in Vietnam and the prolonged strife it had stirred at home.

During the 1968 presidential campaign Richard Nixon had promised war-weary voters that he would "bring the American people together again" and achieve "peace with honor." But he didn't promise a deadline, and the conflict was still not over when the next presidential campaign was heating up. Mindful that voters were still waiting for an end to the Vietnam War, the president stepped up peace talks with the North Vietnamese. Even before an agreement was signed, the public rewarded the president with a landslide victory over Democrat George McGovern (predictably, the Democrat got Mike Stivic's vote, while Archie was a Nixon man). On January 27, 1973, the United States and Hanoi signed a peace agreement, and within two months virtually all of the American troops returned home.

Supporters of the Equal Rights Amendment marched in New York City (above).

brought home to many Americans as never before that leveling the playing field for women was long overdue.

If the number-one feminist heroine of 1973 was the pseudonymous Jane Roe of the abortion case, then tennis champ Billie Jean King was the runner-up. The winner of three straight Wimbledon singles titles in 1966, '67 and '68 and the first female athlete to earn more than $100,000 a year, King accepted a challenge from Bobby Riggs, a 55-year-old former tennis champion who didn't know what he

Just five days before the signing of the peace accords, the Supreme Court handed down an opinion on an issue that was just as divisive as Vietnam. Except for a few circumstances, abortion had been defined as a crime for more than a century. Now, in a stunning reversal, the justices ruled in the case of *Roe v. Wade* that women had a constitutional right to safe and legal abortions. Feminists were jubilant, but many other Americans denounced the ruling on religious grounds. Conservatives saw it as a social threat to the family and an invitation to promiscuity.

Another feminist advance that year was the passage of the Equal Rights Amendment by Congress. Although 63 percent of Americans said they favored its ratification, an organization called STOP ERA galvanized conservative opponents of the amendment, and it failed to win the approval of the 38 state legislatures required for adoption. Nevertheless, the pro-ERA campaign

was in for. In a televised "Battle of the Sexes" that drew an estimated 50,000,000 viewers, the net-charging, power-hitting King trounced Riggs in three straight sets. At the same time, she raised respect for all women athletes to a new level.

Television loomed larger than ever for sports fans. Twenty-eight million people tuned in to the 1973 Kentucky Derby to see for themselves whether Secretariat would live up to his reputation, and football was no longer limited to weekends. Thanks to ABC and National Football League commissioner Pete Rozelle, who came up with the idea of televising weeknight games in prime time, pigskin devotees could settle down in front of the set on Monday nights and forget their worries. The team to watch was the Pittsburgh Steelers. After 40 years of losing, the team underwent a miraculous transformation, thanks to the likes of quarterback Terry Bradshaw and running back Franco Harris, and became the sports juggernaut of the decade.

If the news was good in Steel City, the most ignominious scandal in American history unfolded in Washington, D.C., and at its center stood President Nixon. Although many Americans deplored his policies in Vietnam, in his first term he had promoted social and economic programs that even his more liberal political opponents applauded. Responding to the growing ranks of environmentalists, who in 1970 turned out in full force for the first Earth Day to demonstrate their concern about the state of the planet's health, Nixon signed into law a number of bills that stepped up government efforts to protect the environment. He also backed measures designed to protect blacks and women from discrimination.

Yet for all his forward-looking domestic programs, Nixon had a dark, even paranoid side that would be his downfall. In May 1973 the Senate Select Committee on Presidential Campaign Activities convened a hearing into the events surrounding a break-in at the Democratic National Committee's office in the Watergate complex in Washington, D.C., during the 1972 presidential campaign. Investigators had piled up ample evidence that zealous Nixon partisans had planned to slip in and install bugs so they could eavesdrop on the Democrats. It was one of many "dirty tricks" directed at people judged to be Nixon enemies; the scofflaws had engaged in an assortment of crimes including money-laundering, wiretap-

Howard Cosell of *Monday Night Football* (above) also hosted the King-Riggs match.

ping, bribery and burglary. High officials close to Nixon had been involved in the Watergate break-in, from its planning to the attempted cover-up of the White House connection. One of the insiders, former counsel John Dean, testified against the president, declaring that Nixon had had a direct hand in the cover-up.

But the most electrifying moment came when a White House aide revealed that the president had secretly taped all of his conversations in the Oval Office and on his telephone. The tapes, it seemed, must hold the answer to the critical question posed by Senator Howard Baker of the Select Committee: "What did the president know, and when did he know it?"

For a year Nixon fought off every legal effort to make him hand over the tapes until July 24, 1974, when the Supreme Court ordered him to surrender the tapes. In answer to Baker's question, they revealed that six days after the break-in, the president ordered the CIA to stop the FBI's probe of the matter. The American public was appalled to learn that its president had deliberately obstructed justice. The cry of outrage left Nixon no alternative, and on August 8, he announced that he would resign the following day. His successor, Gerald Ford, optimistically declared that "our long national nightmare" had ended. In fact, the nation would be a long time recovering from the crisis that Nixon's criminal actions and lack of regard for the Constitution triggered. As one disillusioned citizen put it, "After Watergate, it's crazy to have trust in politicians. I'm totally cynical, skeptical.... Someone should have told [Nixon] that this is a democracy, not a monarchy."

America was still absorbing the bitter experience of Watergate when its bicentennial arrived on July 4, 1976, and set off a restorative outburst of flag-waving celebrations all over the country. Though the president had disgraced himself and, by extension, his nation, people were reminded that the United States had endured other crises and had emerged whole.

Americans weren't all gloom and doom, despite the political and social shock waves that had swept the country in recent years. If they couldn't manage a smile on their own, the bright yellow Smiley Face was everywhere, reminding folks to lighten up and have a nice day. In fact, a lot of people *were* having a lot of fun. The rich were playing with the newest electronic toy, the videocassette recorder, which came on the market with a hefty thousand-dollar price tag. Little kids grooved on the friendly neighbors, peppy songs and lovable monsters of public television's *Sesame Street*. A novel educational program designed to get poor children ready for kindergarten, *Sesame Street's* easygoing approach to learning also appealed to middle-class children and their moms and dads.

For legions of young adults looking for a place to play, the destination was the disco, where they gyrated the night away (and sometimes did

John Travolta set a high standard for disco dancers in *Saturday Night Fever* (above).

drugs) to recorded music that was heavy on rhythm and short on lyrical subtlety. Peacock-proud males took to the dance floor in the latest fashions—tight-fitting pants in leather or gaudy plaids, platform shoes or knee-high boots, wide-lapelled suits and opulent shirts of silk or velvet with collars open to show off gold chains. The garb of female partners was equally flashy, featuring clingy fabrics in bright colors and big patterns and thigh-baring skirts.

Meanwhile, the ranks of computer nerds were about to expand tremendously. Until the mid-'70s, computers were the province of the government, corporations, universities and other large institutions. The reason was simple: The least expensive machine, the minicomputer, was well beyond the range of the average consumer since it cost as much as $20,000. Would-be users were eager to secure a share of the computer's power, which was absolutely essential to some of the greatest technological advances of the decade. Among them were the sophisticated techniques of computed tomography, magnetic resonance imaging and ultrasound that made it far easier to diagnose disease and detect internal injuries. The Jupiter-bound spacecraft *Pioneer 10* had multiple systems that mapped its course and controlled not only the scientific instruments it carried but also its communications with the Kennedy Space Center in Florida and the Jet Propulsion Laboratory in Pasadena, California, where engineers monitored *Pioneer's* flight on huge arrays of multiple con-

Heralded by cannons, a fleet of 16 square-rigger ships sailed up New York Harbor on July 4, 1976, before a crowd of six million spectactors (above). "Operation Sail" was one of the nation's most spectacular bicentennial events.

soles. And Boeing Aircraft's new jumbo jet, the 747, was just as dependent on digital processing. A flight management computer calculated the optimum altitude, speed and routing, and a maintenance computer kept constant check on about 70 different systems, while other computers controlled the navigation system and the automatic flight control systems.

In the '60s a handful of cybernetically minded radicals had begun calling for "computer liberation" to bring its power to the people. The device that did it was the personal computer. The first one, called the Altair 8800, was the subject of *Popular Electronics'* cover story in the January '75 issue. Sold by mail as an unassembled kit for $397, it consisted of a box with microchips inside and little light bulbs on the outside that the owner programmed to blink by throwing switches. Blinking was all the Altair 8800 could do, but it was a major breakthrough. A Harvard sophomore and computer wizard named Bill Gates understood how important it was, and he and his friend Paul Allen quickly wrote a program for the Altair 8800

in the widely used computer language BASIC and licensed it to the Altair's manufacturer.

Other start-up companies were peddling PCs of their own, but they appealed only to the small universe of electronics afficionados. In April 1977 two 20-something shoestring entrepreneurs, Stephen Wozniak and Steve Jobs, made history with the Apple II. Designed for the mass market, their user-friendly computer was fully assembled and had a plastic case and a built-in keyboard that gave it reassuring resemblance to an electric typewriter. Data was stored on a cassette recorder, and instead of a dedicated monitor the household TV set was used for displays. At $1,298, the Apple II wasn't cheap, but it was a far cry from the $20,000 minicomputer. Software writers got busy on spreadsheets, word processing and data base applications that widened the market for the PC.

By the close of the decade, computer liberation was a reality. A revolution born of American ingenuity was sweeping the land, and it was becoming a very different place from what it had been only 10 years earlier.

EARTH DAY 1970

It was the biggest show of flower power the country had ever seen. On April 22, 1970, 20 million people gathered at state capitals, college campuses, churches and parks for a nationwide environmental rally. New York's Fifth Avenue was closed to traffic for two hours, while 10,000 people flocked to the Washington Monument and Congress recessed.

Earth Day was the country's first opportunity to voice its growing concern about the dismal state of environmental affairs. Satellite images depicting the earth as a beautiful blue ball floating in space had powerfully reinforced the knowledge that water, land and air were, in fact, finite resources. As the United States neared its 200th birthday it seemed to many people that the country was being inundated by poisons and garbage. Billions of tons of mercury had been dumped into rivers and lakes, rendering them unfit for swimming and fishing; chlorofluorocarbons from refrigerators and aerosols were endangering the ozone layer; 142 tons of smoke billowed into the air every year; 7 million junked cars, 30 million tons of paper, 28 billion bottles and 48 billion cans littered the landscape. The waste of the high-consumption American lifestyle and the effects of 200 years of casual exploitation of natural resources had gone unchecked for too long. (The figures were shocking: With only 4.5 percent of the world's population, the United States consumes some 25 percent of its oil and other resources.)

Before Earth Day, environmental concern was traditionally expressed Teddy Roosevelt-style through the buying of land for national and state parks, forests and wilderness tracts. Environmental ills and threats were simply not the subject of public debate. Concerned about this silence, Wisconsin senator Gaylord Nelson persuaded Presi-

Activists staged the "burial" at left on Earth Day, and in Washington, D.C., a gas mask commented on air pollution (above).

Denis Hayes, shown above addressing a rally in New York City, worked with Senator Gaylord Nelson (near right) to arouse interest in problems like contaminated waterways (right); thousands marched in Washington, D.C. (opposite).

"Earth Day is for the environment what Martin Luther King Day is for civil rights."
—DENIS HAYES, CEO of the Earth Day Network

dent Kennedy to take a five-day conservation tour in 1963. Unfortunately, the tour did little more than pay well-intentioned lip service to the cause. It wasn't until 1969, when antiwar activists were using teach-ins to promote debate on college campuses about the government's Vietnam policies, that Nelson had his epiphany: What was needed was a nationwide teach-in on the environment. Nelson enlisted Denis Hayes, a fiery young environmental activist, and together they raised funds and sent letters and articles to governors, mayors

of major cities, colleges and schools urging them to issue proclamations and organize activities on April 22.

The idea of Earth Day proved immensely popular, as more than 1,000 communities, 2,000 colleges and 10,000 schools took part. Although there were scoffers, the outpouring of support and concern cut across race, class, gender and ideological divides. The events that took place on April 22 included seminars, parades, speeches, concerts, trash cleanups and metal-recycling

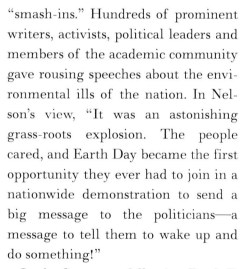

"smash-ins." Hundreds of prominent writers, activists, political leaders and members of the academic community gave rousing speeches about the environmental ills of the nation. In Nelson's view, "It was an astonishing grass-roots explosion. The people cared, and Earth Day became the first opportunity they ever had to join in a nationwide demonstration to send a big message to the politicians—a message to tell them to wake up and do something!"

In the first years following Earth Day, concrete legislative strides were made: The Environmental Protection Agency was established, the Clean Air Act was strengthened and Congress passed the Clean Water Act. Environmental activist groups such as Greenpeace were founded, and the United Nations organized an environmental conference in Stockholm in 1972.

But the greatest achievement of Earth Day 1970 was its mobilizing of mainstream America. In the words of the Audubon Society, "The movement has evolved from a lonely crusade led by scattered clots of zealots and literary-minded philosophers to an extraordinary social and political force whose impact has changed how human beings think, feel and live on the earth."

Aftermath

As Earth Day 2000 draws near, some 80 percent of Americans consider themselves environmentalists, contributing $3 billion annually to 12,000 environmental organizations. More than 40 major federal laws addressing clean air and water, energy conservation, hazardous waste and pesticides have been enacted by Congress since 1970, and recycling has become a household habit.

In 1990 Denis Hayes organized a 20th anniversary global Earth Day. Some 200 million people participated in activities, including the formation of a 500-mile human chain across France. Environmentalists are now preparing for Earth Day 2000 and focusing on a Clean Energy Agenda. Television specials, rallies, concerts and the internet will help bring global participants together as they engage in close to 50,000 events. Thirty years later, the rallying cry of the movement, "Earth Day is Every Day!" has truly become reality.

Newspapers and bottles were collected on Earth Day for recycling (above, and opposite, above); a poster gave environmental problems a global dimension (inset), and a demonstrator concerned about oil spills invited passersby to turn in their gas station credit cards (above, right).

MONDAY NIGHT FOOTBALL

America's love affair with televised professional football was consummated on December 28, 1958, when the Baltimore Colts' bruising fullback Alan Ameche plunged into the end zone with the winning score in overtime of the National Football League championship game. That thriller between the Colts and the New York Giants, which featured 15 future Hall of Famers, was one of the first nationally televised pro football games. It did wonders for the NFL's appeal; by the mid-'60s, America was tuned in every Sunday. In 1967, when the Packers and the Chiefs met in the first Super Bowl, both NBC and CBS televised the game, which generated a combined Nielsen rating of 40.8 and attracted 85 million viewers.

So it was somewhat surprising that when the NFL's forward-thinking commissioner, Pete Rozelle, approached the networks in 1970 with the idea of televising a weeknight, prime-time pro football game, they balked. NBC was raking in viewers with *Laugh-In* on Monday nights, and CBS had a ratings winner in *The Doris Day Show.* "Preempt Doris Day?" CBS president Bob Wood reportedly asked. "Are you out of your mind?"

Well, as Ms. Day would have said, *Que sera, sera:* ABC, which was then a distant third in the ratings, took the handoff from the NFL and ran, creating not only its most consistent ratings earner but also an American institution in the process. Indeed, ABC hasn't reached the end zone yet—at 30 years and counting, *Monday Night Football* is the second-longest running show on television, after *60 Minutes.*

ABC executive Roone Arledge was the driving force behind *Monday Night Football,* and his team introduced several elements that contributed to the show's smashing success. With only one game a week to prepare for, ABC focused all of its energies on making that game

For 10 seasons, the team of Meredith, Cosell and Gifford (opposite, left to right) was a fixture in U.S. stadiums (above).

a major event. Monday night broadcasts had all manner of bells and whistles. Whereas Sunday afternoon contests were shot by four or five cameras, ABC would use nine on Monday nights. To get the viewer up-close-and-personal with the action, the network placed handheld cameras on each sideline, and to give folks at home a more commanding perspective, ABC arranged to have the now-famous Goodyear blimp puttering high above the stadium, beaming stirring overhead shots to the nation. Reverse-angle shots, split-screen replays and in-depth player profiles would debut in years to come on *Monday Night Football.*

In addition to its technological innovations, ABC broke with tradition in the broadcast

Assembled by Arledge (opposite, left), the original broadcasting trio of Cosell, Jackson and Meredith (inset, left to right) announced the first Monday night telecast on September 21, 1970, a regular-season game in which Joe Namath (No. 12, below), Matt Snell (No. 41) and the rest of the New York Jets lost 31–21 to the Cleveland Browns.

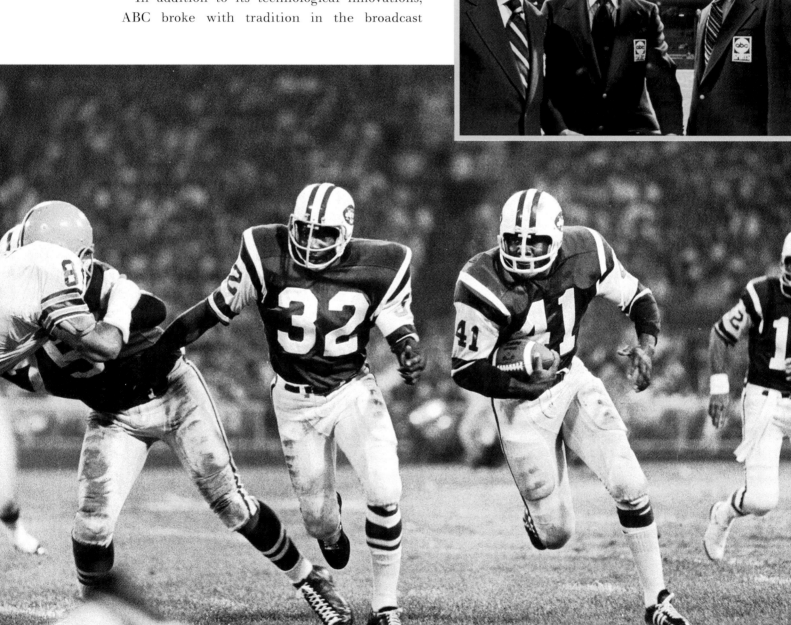

booth, where it placed three commentators instead of the usual two. The interplay between this trio—the entertainingly bombastic Howard Cosell, the good ol' boy former Dallas Cowboys quarterback Don Meredith and, for the first season, the play-by-play announcer Keith Jackson—was often as entertaining as the game on the field. (In *Monday Night Football*'s second season, ex-NFL great Frank Gifford replaced Jackson, who shifted to college football.) Cosell and Meredith had the charged chemistry of polar opposites, and the former, with his unvarnished opinions and signature nasal delivery, became a household name. Some Americans

> ## "It's like a mini-Super Bowl every week. There's a tremendous sense in the city and among the players that the spotlight is now shining on you."
>
> *—AL MICHAELS, play-by-play announcer for ABC's* **Monday Night Football**

may have found him abrasive, but Cosell, who passed away in 1995, remains a giant in sports broadcasting. His highlights show at halftime of *MNF* broadcasts, wherein he established his trademark "He. Could. Go. All. The. Way." line—currently echoed in tribute by ABC and ESPN's Chris Berman—became an industry touchstone. He was also part of two landmark *Monday Night Football* moments: On December 9, 1974, he interviewed John Lennon in the *MNF* booth (incredibly, Ronald Reagan was the other halftime guest), and six years later, he broke the news of Lennon's assassination to a national audience.

Though no one could have predicted the overwhelming success of *Monday Night Football*, ABC received an early sign that it was on the right track with its groundbreaking program. After the Cleveland Browns defeated Joe Namath's New York Jets 31–21 in the show's September 21, 1970, debut, the network was flooded with angry letters from both Jets fans and from Browns fans, each accusing Cosell of bias against their beloved team. "Then," said NFL senior vice president for broadcasting Dennis Lewin, who was ABC's replay producer on the telecast, "we knew we had done something right."

Among the many technological innovations introduced by *Monday Night Football* were moving field-level cameras that tracked the action from behind the benches (left) and roving hand-held cameras that captured the off-the-field reactions of cheerleaders (above) and players on the bench (below).

Aftermath

ABC's *Monday Night Football* cracked the top 25 in the Nielsen ratings during its second season on the air. The most successful and longest-running prime-time sports series in television history, *MNF* enters its 30th season in 1999 and has never been stronger. *MNF* is the No. 1 show on the ABC Network and currently ranks fifth among all prime-time shows.

ABC Sports, which pioneered super slow-motion replays and the use of state-of-the-art graphics, will continue to innovate in '99 as it broadcasts each game in High-Definition Television and adds the "First and 10" electronic first-down line. *MNF* will also feature "Enhanced TV," with on-line programming tied to the game broadcast in real time.

Al Michaels, television's top football play-by-play voice, returns in '99 for his 14th season as the *MNF* announcer. He will be joined by former All-Pro quarterback Boomer Esiason, who begins his second season behind the microphone.

JUMBO JETS

In the early hours of January 22, 1970, Pan American Airlines' new plane, *Clipper Victor*, took off from New York's John F. Kennedy airport bound for London. The takeoff was some six hours late, but far from being upset about the delay, the passengers were in a festive mood, since this was the first flight of the much anticipated Boeing 747 jumbo jet. One traveler recalled that after a lavish buffet with a well-stocked bar, "most of us walked halfway across the Atlantic, strolling through the airplane, exploring the luxurious first-class space, the elegant upper deck, and peeking into the busy flight deck area where the business of flying the airplane was being conducted." Even Fidel Castro couldn't resist taking a peek when a hijacker took over a 747 and forced it to fly to Havana in August 1970. Castro admired the aircraft and chatted with the pilots about its amazing capacity and features before letting the largest plane ever

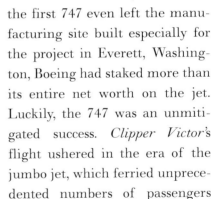

to land in Cuba fly back to Miami.

Surprisingly, though, during the four years of its design and development, Boeing feared that it might end up with a white elephant on its hands. The financial risks were enormous, and before the first 747 even left the manufacturing site built especially for the project in Everett, Washington, Boeing had staked more than its entire net worth on the jet. Luckily, the 747 was an unmitigated success. *Clipper Victor*'s flight ushered in the era of the jumbo jet, which ferried unprecedented numbers of passengers around the globe and revolutionized air travel.

The roots of the jumbo jet stretch back to World War II, when Germany alarmed the Allies by launching the technologically advanced Messerschmitt Ne 262 Schwalbe, a jet fighter with wings swept back like a swallow's. When Allied troops advanced into Germany, a team of American aeronautical engineers and physicists organized by the

Since its initial production line (left), Boeing has built nearly 1,250 747s; 2.2 billion passengers have flown on the jetliner (above).

U.S. Strategic Air Force was right behind them, on the trail of scientific treasure. The search party found what it was looking for at the Reichsmarshal Hermann Goering Aeronautical Research Institute 100 miles east of Berlin: boxes filled with papers describing the wind-tunnel research used in designing the revolutionary swept wings of the Messerschmitt. Three of the engineers on the team were from Boeing, and the company quickly learned about the German research, which one historian called "the equivalent of an aerospace Holy Grail to Boeing."

Boeing, which had recently built a $750,000 wind tunnel of its own, was in a prime position to exploit the concept of a jet plane with wings swept back at angles between 35 and 40 degrees. During the Cold War years the company built the B-47 and B-52 bombers, and it also produced the comparatively small 707, 727 and 737 commercial jetliners—all forebears to the 747.

American prosperity grew apace after the war, and by the 1960s the booming economy had created a generation of well-heeled globetrotters so large that the airlines couldn't keep up with their

On September 30, 1968, Boeing employees, airline customers and the press gathered for the rollout of the 747 (opposite), which was the first airplane wide enough to require two aisles (above); the cockpit (left) was set back from the nose inside the hump atop the plane that gave it its distinctive profile.

"Boeing airplanes change the world and bring people, ideas and opportunities together, increasing global understanding and prosperity. The 747 is at the heart of the legacy."

—*ALAN MULALLY, president, Boeing Commercial Airplanes Group*

urge to travel; the 707 accommodated a mere 141 passengers. In 1965, airline powerhouse Pan Am threatened to take its business to the competition if Boeing didn't come up with a new high-capacity, high-speed design.

The 747 was initially conceived as an aircraft that could be easily converted from a passenger plane to a cargo plane once the supersonic jet took over as the premier commercial carrier, as the industry expected. (Ironically, by the time the first supersonic passenger plane, the *Concorde*, went into service in 1976, concerns about its effects on the environment and exorbitant fuel costs ensured that only the ultra-rich would fly at the speed of sound.)

The 747's director of engineering, Joe Sutter, firmly resisted Pan Am's demand for a full-size upper deck because it would compromise safety during an evacuation. "Of all the decisions we made," Sutter said, "the most important was selecting the wide single deck. It gave us an airplane that was efficient and extremely flexible and was one of the main reasons for its success."

When Sutter's design and production team—nicknamed "The Incredibles" for their breakneck, round-the-clock schedule—finished the first 747, their pride was immense, for they had created the largest plane ever built. It had a 231-foot aluminum body, a 196-foot wingspan and a maximum take-off weight of 710,000 pounds, and it could fly as many as 5,300 miles before refueling. The plane carried up to 366 passengers, more than two and a half times as many as the 707.

The drawback of the jumbo jet, if there is one, is emotional rather than technical: Passengers now take long-distance travel completely for granted. As one *Newsweek* magazine correspondent lamented recently, "Forget the romance of flight—Lindbergh, Amelia Earhart and Antoine de Saint-Exupéry. Man's conquest of the air leads directly to a fat, unsexy airplane that was designed to make air travel as predictable, and predictably commercial, as riding on a city bus."

Aftermath

The Boeing 747 family of jets has dominated long-distance air travel for some 30 years, flying 2.2 billion people a distance greater than 42,000 trips to the moon and back. Retired 747s starred in action movies such as *Airport*, and NASA has used the plane to carry space shuttles between landing and launch sites.

The latest 747-400 flies 3,000 miles farther than the original 747, and its state-of-the-art flight deck can be flown by two pilots instead of three. It remains the world's fastest subsonic commercial jetliner and offers airlines the lowest seat-mile cost of any jetliner in history.

Boeing is now the world's largest aerospace company, building not only commercial jetliners and supersonic military fighters but also rockets, helicopters and satellites. The company is the prime contractor on the International Space Station and operates the space shuttle for NASA.

Flight attendants from the airlines flying 747s put on a uniform fashion show (opposite); the 747 was the only plane big enough to transport the space shuttle between its landing and launch sites (top); first-class lounges (above) were turned into revenue-producing seating space after the 1973 oil crisis caused fuel prices to rise.

SESAME STREET

"Sunny day, sweepin' the clouds away/ On my way, to where the air is sweet/ Can you tell me how to get ... how to get to *Sesame Street?*" So began the first installment of *Sesame Street* on November 10, 1969—with a question; and before long, nearly everyone in America under the age of four could provide the answer to that question, and many others.

At first glance, Sesame Street did not look like a place children would flock to. Set among apartment buildings, a playground and a corner store, it seemed only ordinary. Its residents, though, were anything but. They included fuzzy blue monsters, talking frogs and an 8-foot-2-inch bird; they were unusually friendly, and they always seemed excited about learning new things.

The person who put *Sesame Street* on the map was Joan Ganz Cooney. She had produced documentaries about inner-city education, and in 1968 she decided to try a new approach to the issue.

Cooney founded the Children's Television Workshop to produce educational programming for children—particularly poor urban children with few resources to help them prepare for school. At the time television had never been used for educational purposes. Cooney and her colleagues were in uncharted, even revolutionary, territory. Indeed, the project began as experimental research and ended as a cultural landmark, a groundbreaking television show that helped kids to learn. Knowing that preschool children watched a great deal of television, Cooney decided to use the hallmarks of kid's TV—slapstick humor, music and the fast-paced techniques of commercials—to teach children about letters and numbers.

As the program's "sponsors," letters and numbers have a prominent place, but teaching children to recognize and use symbols is only one part of *Sesame Street*'s mission. The show's educators also aimed to develop children's cognitive

Children hung out on Sesame Street with Big Bird and Mr. Snuffleupagus (left) and learned to read with Grover (above).

Big Bird © The Jim Henson Company; Sesame Street is a trademark of Children's Television Workshop.

processes such as reasoning and problem-solving, and they wanted to teach children about their physical and social environment.

According to a longtime producer and director of the show, the program's creators "didn't want another clubhouse or treasure house or tree-house...[but rather] a real inner-city street, and we should populate it with real people." In keeping with that proposal, the children appearing on the program came from the schools and neighborhoods of New York City, where the show's studios are located. The show's original professional cast—the shopkeeper, Mr. Hooper; the music teacher, Bob; the

nurse, Susan; and the teacher, Gordon—was selected with the help of children. *Sesame Street* also successfully tackled the issue of physically and mentally challenged persons by featuring them regularly on the show. In fact, Linda Bove, who is deaf, has played the longest-running role of any physically challenged person in a television series. *Sesame Street* broke further new ground as the first preschool program to feature a multicultural cast, and the show remains an inclusive place where children can see others similar to themselves.

Probably nothing endeared the program to children as much as Jim Henson's Muppets,

"C is for Cookie, that's good enough for me....Oh, Cookie, Cookie, Cookie, starts with C."

—COOKIE MONSTER'S SONG, with words and music by Joe Raposo

Early residents of Sesame Street included Bob (top, with children), Maria and Luis (right) and Mr. Hooper (above); Mr. Hooper, Gordon, Oscar the Grouch, Bob and Susan (opposite, left to right) made learning fun.

Henson (far right, top) populated Sesame Street with Muppets Ernie and Bert (left), Oscar the Grouch (above) and Ker- mit the Frog, shown at right with Susan; a graphic lesson taught children the alphabet (far right, center).

which get their name from the fact that they are operated as both marionettes and hand puppets. Henson's creatures had been appearing in commercials, on *The Ed Sullivan Show* and on their own five-minute late-night program, *Sam and Friends*, since the mid-'50s. They are distinct from *Sesame Street*, but the Muppets first found stardom on the show. From the jokester Ernie and his square roommate, Bert, who live in the basement of 123 Sesame Street, to Oscar the Grouch, whose home is a garbage can next to the stoop of Bert and Ernie's apartment building, the Muppets are as varied in character as the humans in the neighborhood. Some represent children at a particular stage of development, including the earnest and lovable Grover, the inquisitive Big Bird and the single-minded Cookie Monster. And, of course, the role of the always reasonable adult of the bunch more often than not fell to Kermit

the Frog, voiced by Henson.

Because of *Sesame Street*, children began arriving in kindergarten knowing more than their parents or older brothers and sisters had. Research has proven the show's effectiveness as a learning tool, and as the program challenged schools to expand their curricula, it expanded its own curriculum. For example, the numbers taught on the show grew from 1–10 to 1–40, and difficult subjects were sometimes presented. When actor Will Lee died in 1982, so did his character, Mr. Hooper. Children also learned about love, marriage and birth when Maria and Luis married and had a baby.

As the author of *Sesame Street Unpaved* said in 1998, "*Sesame Street* isn't just a TV show—it's a very special place. It's a place we go where monsters, animals, numbers, letters and humans of every size, shape and color live together and share in the joys and sorrows and laughter of life."

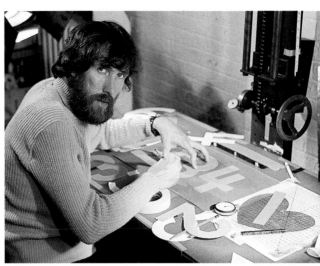

Aftermath

Celebrating its 30th anniversary in 1998, *Sesame Street* is aired in more than 140 nations and has won 75 Emmys, more than any other television program. Since *Sesame Street*'s launch, Children's Television Workshop has produced various programs, including *The Electric Company*, *3-2-1 Contact*, *Square One TV* and *Big Bag*.

   CTW's latest production is *Dragon Tales*, an animated series designed to encourage kids to approach new experiences with confidence. Thirty years and counting—CTW continues to set the standard for educating and entertaining children and families around the world.

THE BICENTENNIAL

Booming cannons heralded the entry of 15 majestic ships into New York Harbor as 20,000 small boats bobbed in their wake and six million onlookers lined the banks to witness the spectacular scene. Another 200 naval vessels joined the flotilla as it sailed up the Hudson River. These grand and graceful ships (square-riggers with masts reaching up to 127 feet) had sailed from all over the world to join Americans in celebrating the country's 200th birthday.

Operation Sail, as the parade of tall ships was called, was only one of the many events that marked the nation's bicentennial on July 4, 1976. Battles of the Revolutionary and Civil Wars were refought, Paul Revere's ride was reenacted—not just from Lexington to Concord—but all across the country. The American Freedom Train (a steam locomotive pulling 25 railroad cars) brought bicentennial exhibits to 137 cities. A total of 10,000 new citizens were naturalized in joyful mass ceremonies as bells pealed all across the nation at precisely two in the afternoon. Every town and city worth its salt had a parade. But Philadelphia's—in which a six-hour marathon entertained two million onlookers with hundreds of ethnic groups in full regalia—was definitely the crowning glory. Meanwhile, 22 miles away in Valley Forge, President Ford was on hand to welcome a train of Conestoga wagons and prairie schooners as they completed a two-year odyssey through 48 states. Along the way, thousands of would-be settlers rode with the train for a day or two just for a taste of the pioneer days. Droves of cyclists came out for the "Bikecentennial 76" ride held along the converted transcontinental highway; log-rolling contests were held in Alaska; and Dixieland jazz festivals were the order of the day in New Orleans. Philadelphia baked a five-story-high, red-white-and-blue chocolate cake weighing a fattening 49,000 pounds and (after due admiration) distributed it to charities. Fireworks—like parades

From Portland, Oregon (left), to Washington, D.C. (above), Americans celebrated the bicentennial in creative ways.

35

The bicentennial celebrations included the entrance of the tall ships into New York Harbor (opposite), Revolutionary War costumes in Philadelphia (below) and, all across the land, throngs of cheering crowds (left).

'America turned the corner on Sunday on a self-induced illness of the spirit and stretched its psyche in a burst of national joy and celebration.'

—THE BIRMINGHAM NEWS, *July 1976*

and cookouts—were also ubiquitous, with Washington, D.C., leading the nation in an orgy of celestial explosions valued at $200,000.

Initially, Congress had considered creating a 50-state network of bicentennial parks, but the exorbitant price tag caused them to encourage locally organized celebrations instead. The plan to create "a neighborhood effort without a world's fair centerpiece" proved an extremely popular and farsighted move. Towns and cities, small and large, rallied to the occasion and organized activities celebrating the past, present and future of the United States. Each state had its own bicentennial commission with a federal committee providing $11 million in matching funds for an incredible

200,000 events. The bicentennial symbol, a five-pointed star surrounded by red, white and blue stripes, adorned practically every corner of the festival. Amazingly, the Fourth of July events made up only five percent of the total bicentennial effort. Historic renovations, archaeological digs, museum exhibitions, teaching materials, books, plays and films made up a portion of the rest.

In the end it was television that truly brought "the largest volunteer movement in peacetime history" home to the nation. As a journalist from the Tulsa, Oklahoma, *Daily World* summed it up, "TV gave us a sense of drama and sweep, of the American oneness out of diversity and the remembrance of where we have been and what we have done."

Such an outpouring of national celebration was hardly expected given the widespread malaise of the early '70s. In the space of a few years, Americans had lost a war for the first time, suffered their first gas crisis and had a president resign. But the emphasis on grass-roots organizing urged people to focus on what they were proud of: their ethnic heritage, the historic role their town had played, the unique music produced by one region, the delicious food from another—the list went on.

Aftermath

One legacy of what Walter Cronkite called "the greatest, most colossal birthday party in 200 years" was—not surprisingly—a resurgence in patriotism. The Reagan era's insistent focus on America's limitless future was built upon the bicentennial spirit and proved to be a salve for a demoralized nation.

The bicentennial's more tangible legacy lies in our recovery of the past. Dozens of scholarship efforts and archaeological digs launched as part of the celebration helped shed further light on America, the complexities of its past and its legacy as the oldest surviving democratic republic on earth.

In 1973, concerned about alienating and marginalizing minorities, the bicentennial organizers held a three-day conference in Arizona inviting Native Americans to discuss their rather ambivalent response to America's 200th birthday. Projects were proposed to improve tribal facilities, and in the end, 38 tribes decided to participate in an effort to celebrate their own cultural identity and to promote better understanding among all Americans. Also as part of the bicentennial celebration, sites of historic importance to African Americans were added to the National Register, while another 156 programs involving African Americans were funded.

At day's end *Time* captured the mood: "It was an altogether fitting celebration of the 200th anniversary of America's independence and perhaps the best part of it was that its supreme characteristics were good will, good humor and after a long night of paralyzing self-doubt, good feelings about the U.S."

DOG DAY AFTERNOON  15738

Clint Eastwood
Dirty Harry 15442

ROCKY  M205712 VHS hi-fi

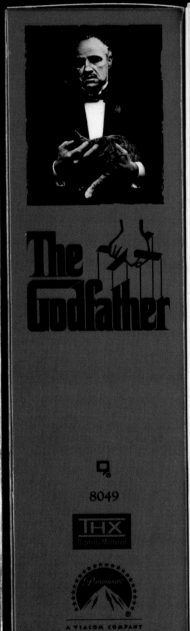The Godfather 8049 THX A VIACOM COMPANY

The JERK  VHS HI FI 66005

ANNIE HALL M200251 VHS hi-fi

JAWS  VHS HI FI 82582

BLAZING SADDLES 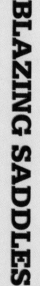 1001

VCR

The videocassette recorder (VCR) is such a common household item—nearly as prevalent as the television, which is in 98 percent of American homes—that it's easy forget how much of a novelty the machine was when it first appeared, and how much controversy surrounded that appearance.

When Sony's Betamax home video recorder debuted in the mid-'70s, many consumers were mystified by the machine. They did not understand that its videotape could be played back instantly, and that VCRs could be set to record TV programs unattended. Customers in home electronics stores asked questions such as, "Where do I get the picture developed?"

This was a problem Sony's ad-men relished. They solved it with a series of witty TV commercials, including one in which Count Dracula returned to his lair before dawn, turned on his Betamax and intoned in thick Transylvanian

VCRs Transform Entertainment

cadences, "If you work nights the way I do, you miss a lot of great TV shows. But I don't miss them anymore, thanks to Sony's Betamax deck which hooks up to any TV set. While I am out, Betamax is automatically videotaping my favorite show for me to play back when I get home. And now I'm going to watch it."

Its horror-movie milieu notwithstanding, this commercial was never intended to scare anyone. Yet it gave Sidney Sheinberg, the president of Universal Pictures, the heebie-jeebies. He saw the home-video recorder as a threat to his industry, a ravenous copyright infringer, and he wanted to stop it. In November 1976, two months after Sheinberg first saw advertisements for the Betamax, Universal Pictures sued Sony on the grounds that the company's distribution of a machine that copied programs off the air made Sony responsible for any copyright violations resulting from its use. With typ-

A novelty in the '70s, the videocassette recorder (above) made it easy for movie fans to see all the decade's great flicks (left).

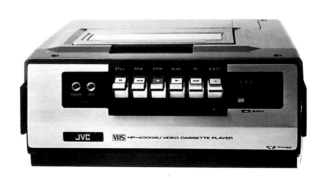

In 1962, a woman demonstrated an early video system that used an ordinary audiotape recorder (above); the JVC model below had a sleeker profile than its boxy forebear at left; the Panasonic at right was a luxury item, selling for about $1,000.

What makes Reggie run in slow motion, high speed or freeze frame?

The Panasonic Omnivision VHS video recorder with wireless remote.

Now you can do what baseball managers have never done—control Reggie Jackson's every move. You can do it with the new Panasonic Omnivision PV-1770 6-hour programmable video recorder. And do it by remote control.

You can make Reggie run fast, slow or stop in his tracks. Because this Omnivision with 4 video heads has Omniflex—special effects that play a picture from as fast as 2 times to as slow as 1/30th normal speed. It'll even show you a freeze frame or one frame at a time.

To give you control over what you see there's Omnisearch. It lets you breeze past the plays that don't interest you to find the exact one that does. And Omnisearch and Omniflex are controlled with the wireless remote, so you'll have Reggie under your thumb.

And for ultimate control, this Omnivision is programmable. It can automatically record 8 different shows over 14 days. You won't miss out on any of the action even when you go out. It also has a 105-channel tuner so you can even record cable programs. However, a cable converter is required for stations scrambled by your cable company.

There's only one thing you'll find uncontrollable: The fun you'll have watching the new Panasonic PV-1770. *TV picture simulated.*

Panasonic.
just slightly ahead of our time.

"Now you don't have to miss *Kojak* because you're watching *Columbo* (or vice versa)...."

—*Videocassette recorder advertisement from 1976*

ical Hollywood understatement, Sheinberg likened Sony's role to that of a gun dealer who sells a weapon to a customer saying, "Feel free to use this gun to kill people."

There was no bloodshed in the VCR's struggle to emerge, but Universal's lawsuit would drag on for seven years—through appeal and all the way to the U.S. Supreme Court, where it was settled in 1984 in Sony's favor. By that time, however, Sheinberg's claim was moot. Even if he had won his suit, VCRs were in so many homes that a ban on their use would have been unenforceable.

But we've fast-forwarded to the closing credits; let's rewind to 1956, when the Ampex Corporation of Redwood City, California, invented the first video recording machine, thereby freeing television from the pressures and limits of live programming. Shows could now be recorded on video, edited and aired at any time. The Ampex recorder was far from being fit for home use—it was massive and cost $50,000—but it spurred Japanese and American home electronics firms to try to adapt it for the mass market. By the mid-'60s several firms had made progress, but it wasn't until 1971 and Sony's invention of the U-Matic that a real breakthrough was achieved. The U-Matic, which became the standard for institutional use, was still too large and expensive for home use, but its core design characteristics were top flight. They became the prototype for the two home VCR formats that would emerge in mid-decade, the Betamax and the VHS systems.

The U-Matic also indirectly prevented a standard format from emerging in the home VCR market. In the early '70s Sony was developing a smaller VCR but shelved these plans in order to back the U-Matic as the industry standard. This was a compromise Sony felt prevented it from getting an edge in the home VCR market. When that market expanded to global proportions, Sony refused to compromise its Betamax design and was reluctant to agree on an industry standard, lest it dilute its brand name or lose out on the benefits of its own technological innovations.

This protectionism proved fatal in the home VCR competition: Sony failed to cultivate support and licensees for its Betamax design, and by the end of 1978 its primary competitors, Victor Company of Japan (JVC) and its parent company, Matsushita, had soundly defeated Sony in the race to establish a standard for VCRs and the prerecorded cassettes that play in them. By decade's end, Betamaxes had gone the way of the 8-Track tape, and the VHS home-video boom was a multi-million-dollar business.

Aftermath

Sony issued its last Betamax in 1984, by which time the VHS format's dominance was complete. Betamax machines and tapes became increasingly rare while their VHS counterparts boomed. The VCR was one of the most popular appliances in the 1980s, and by late 1988 there was one in every two American homes, with the VHS format outselling Beta by a 9 to 1 ratio.

As the '90s dawned home video became a multibillion-dollar industry, video stores dotted every city and town in the country and VCRs, equipped with improved features, continued to sell briskly. In 1994 1.4 million VCRs were sold in the U.S., a 10.6 percent increase over the previous year. By mid-decade, 82.5 percent of American households owned one or more VCRs.

New formats such as laser disks and digital videodisks (DVDs) emerged but by decade's end none appeared capable of unseating the VCR, or the VHS format, as king of the home-video industry.

SECRETARIAT

Horse racing is all about speed, endurance, power and strategy. Fractions of a second are paramount, stamina is a prerequisite; synergy between man and animal, essential. Secretariat, the 1973 Triple Crown winner, embodied each of those qualities. The horse was speed incarnate, could run forever and was smart as a whip.

"There is a whopper," proclaimed Howard M. Gentry, an attendant at the birth of the chestnut foal just after midnight on March 30, 1970, at the Meadow Stud Farm north of Richmond, Virginia. Later the foal would be called "too good-looking to run," "built like a bulldozer," "sexy" and, to those who knew him best, "Red." The world would know him in 1973, though, as Secretariat, the first Triple Crown winner in 25 years.

As a youngster, he occupied the Meadow Farm stall designated for the year's most promising colt yearling and started his training in early August

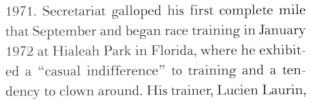

1971. Secretariat galloped his first complete mile that September and began race training in January 1972 at Hialeah Park in Florida, where he exhibited a "casual indifference" to training and a tendency to clown around. His trainer, Lucien Laurin, said, "He's big, awkward and doesn't know what to do with himself." Still, jockeys and exercise boys enjoyed riding him and sensed his superior capabilities. They noticed his precocious intelligence and marveled at his impeccable physique: deep shoulders, a sloping rump and a reddish, almost copper coat that highlighted his musculature.

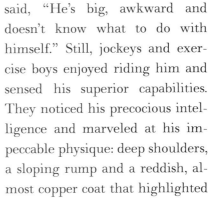

Secretariat raced for the first time on July 4, 1972, at Aqueduct in New York. A 3-to-1 favorite, Red finished fourth, never recovering from a nasty collision and subsequent tangle-up out of the gate. The colt was also slow out of the starting gate at his second race 11 days later, but he charged down the backstretch to take the lead and win by six

Secretariat (above, far right, at the start of the Belmont) and Penny Tweedy (opposite) charmed the nation in 1973.

Secretariat™ Thoroughbred Owners & Breeders Association, Lexington, KY.

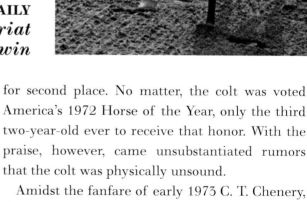

"His only point of reference is himself."

—*CHARLES HATTON,*
former columnist of the DAILY
RACING FORM *on Secretariat*
after the 1973 Triple Crown win

lengths. Impressed, former prizefighter turned Baltimore handicapper Clem Florio inaugurated Secretariat "my Derby horse for next year." The chain of victories racked up by the red colt of Meadow Farm would make him a lot of other people's favorite as well.

Secretariat gained national attention in Saratoga at the Hopeful Stakes in August, rocketing from last to first and winning by five lengths. Wins in the Futurity and the Garden State Stakes followed, but he ran into trouble in the Champagne Stakes where his win (only ⅖ of a second off the track record) was disallowed because he bumped another horse. Secretariat had to settle

for second place. No matter, the colt was voted America's 1972 Horse of the Year, only the third two-year-old ever to receive that honor. With the praise, however, came unsubstantiated rumors that the colt was physically unsound.

Amidst the fanfare of early 1973 C. T. Chenery, the owner of Meadow Farm, died and his daughter, Penny Tweedy, who had taken over the running of the farm in his declining years, was faced with millions in inheritance taxes. Tweedy decided to syndicate her red colt. Four of the 32 shares were retained by Tweedy and a family corporation; the remaining 28 sold quickly at $190,000 a share. Worth more than $6 million, Secretariat would

Secretariat won the Kentucky Derby (opposite) and the Preakness (far right) by the relatively modest margin of 2½ lengths, but his 31-length margin of victory at the Belmont (above) is the widest in Triple Crown history.

prove even more talented than those early investors could have imagined.

Three-year-old Secretariat arrived at the 1973 Kentucky Derby by way of New York, where he ran in the Bay Shore, the Gotham and the Wood, winning the former two and placing third in the latter.

As the Derby approached, speculation about the horse's stamina and the health of his knees added to the pre-race tension and excitement. By post time Churchill Downs was abuzz with more than 137,000 people; another 28 million tuned in from home. Luckily, Secretariat was oblivious to the pressure. After the starting bell, in a decision that would be repeated in all three Triple Crown races, jockey Ron Turcotte let Secretariat set his own pace. The colt began to make his move at the clubhouse turn when a minor bump

against another horse nearly knocked him off pace. Recomposed, Secretariat glided past horse after horse with more grace than Turcotte had ever felt his ride exhibit. "The clumsiness had gone out of him," the jockey said afterward. The pair floated from last to fifth and then from fifth to first—completing each consecutive quarter-mile at a faster pace than the preceding one—and won the race by 2½ lengths. Secretariat's time of 1:59⅖ for the 1¼-mile course remains the Derby record.

On to the Preakness Stakes in Baltimore, where Laurin and Turcotte decided to repeat their Derby strategy: Let the horse lead. After a sluggish start, Secretariat took the lead at the first turn, launching past the leader, Ecole Etage. Within seconds the horse grabbed the second jewel in the coveted Triple Crown in a blazing 1:54⅖. Two down, one to go.

The Belmont Stakes was run three weeks later in Long Island on June 9, in front of 50 million television viewers. Laurin predicted a win by 10 lengths. In the interim, Secretariat had appeared on the covers of *Time, Newsweek* and *Sports Illustrated* and been stalked by photographers like a movie star while Penny Tweedy played horse racing's spokesperson on radio and television programs. Once again, Laurin and Turcotte let Secretariat call the shots. Uncharacteristically, the horse bolted immediately out of the gate. Before long, the clock was Secretariat's only competitor as the horse increased his lead: 28, 29, 30 and finally 31 lengths to set another track—and all-time 1½-mile—record of 2:24. The Triple Crown victory sent shares in Secretariat skyrocketing to $500,000 apiece and put him on pace to earn more than $850,000 by year's end. The red clown of the Meadow Stable became an instant legend: Little girls wrote him congratulatory letters, Sonny and Cher wanted the horse on their show, a Las Vegas casino pursued him to make daily appearances. A bona fide star, Secretariat signed on as a client of that talent stable, the William Morris Agency. Proving himself to be more than a one-trick pony, Secretariat not only burned up the track but also charmed the world.

Secretariat (left, training at Belmont Park) was speed incarnate, a conclusion supported by his wins at the Preakness, the Kentucky Derby and the Belmont (above, left to right); just minutes before being saddled for the Belmont (below), Secretariat was the picture of equine poise.

Aftermath

Apart from merchandising ventures, Penny Tweedy kept Secretariat off television and out of the casinos. Tweedy knew horses. And although she had an exceptional one, perhaps the best ever, she knew that the chances of serious injury on the track or on some promotional appearance were just too high. After capping his career in 1973 with another Horse of the Year award and a win at the Canadian International Championship, Secretariat was retired to stud at Claiborne Farm in Paris, Kentucky. He sired more than 650 offspring, including 57 stakes winners, while fetching stud fees of $75,000 to go with the $1.3 million he earned from racing.

Two other horses would capture the Triple Crown in the 1970s, Seattle Slew in '77 and Affirmed in '78, but neither was as fast as Secretariat. The century would end without another Triple Crown winner.

Secretariat was put down on October 2, 1989, after a bout with laminitis, a hoof disease. His Kentucky Derby and Belmont track records have stood for more than 26 years.

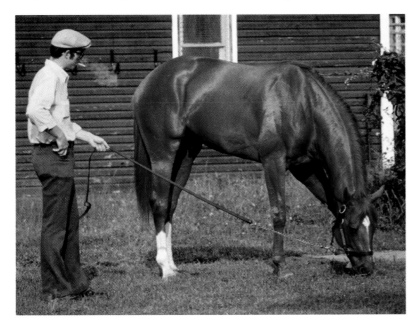

PIONEER 10

On March 2, 1972, *Pioneer 10*, a small unmanned spacecraft tucked inside a 10-foot shroud of a rocket, was launched from Cape Canaveral, Florida, into the great beyond after three days of high winds and delay. Once the fuel was exhausted, *Pioneer 10* shed the rocket like a snakeskin, gliding on toward Jupiter at a brisk 31,114 miles per hour, the greatest velocity ever for a spacecraft.

A six-by-nine-inch aluminum plaque was bolted to *Pioneer 10's* frame. Created at the urging of world-renowned astronomer Carl Sagan of Cornell University, the plaque was like an interstellar ID card that had posed a difficult problem—how to communicate the spacecraft's origins to curious extraterrestrials? The solution was a puzzle, part scientific and part pictorial. A naked man and woman, the man with his hand raised in greeting, stand in front of an outline of *Pioneer 10*, which lends a sense of scale. At the center of the plaque 14 lines radiate from the sun to indicate the levels of solar radiation and give clues to the sun's age. This would indicate the era in which *Pioneer 10* was launched. The solar system, Earth's place in it and *Pioneer's* trajectory are etched across the bottom. The atomic symbol for hydrogen, the most common element in the universe, was etched into the plaque's upper left corner. But this "message-in-a-bottle" gesture remains largely symbolic for earthlings of this era since *Pioneer 10* isn't expected to reach the nearest galaxy for at least 30,000 years. But, as the late Dr. Sagan might have argued, hedging *Pioneer's* bets couldn't hurt.

At times *Pioneer 10's* story seems to come straight from a *Star Trek* episode. It is by far the most famous and far-ranging member of its enterprising family. The first *Pioneer* escaped Earth's gravity in 1958, while *Pioneers 6* through *9* collected data on solar winds, and *Pioneer Venus* mapped the surface of its namesake. Though its builders natu-

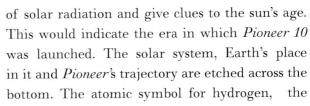

Pioneer 10, shown at left during its final checkout, bore a message to other worlds on an aluminum plaque (above, at rear).

rally hoped it would go farther, No. 10 was designed for a 21-month mission to Jupiter. All too little was known about this brightly colored behemoth of the outer planets, measuring 83,270 miles from pole to pole, compared with the Earth's 7,890. Until then the closest glimpses of Jupiter had been provided by airborne optical and infrared telescopes. Scientists did know that Jupiter was surrounded by extreme radiation and lay beyond an asteroid belt—a formidable stretch of rocky fragments between the orbits of Mars and Jupiter. Most likely the scattered debris of a former planet, the asteroids range from microscopic bits up to several miles in diameter. What the scientists didn't know was the density of the asteroid belt.

In order for *Pioneer 10* to reach Jupiter within our lifetime, the craft could weigh no more than 650 pounds; the engineers and scientists were able to get its weight down to a trim 570 pounds. Because its distance from the sun would rapidly increase and solar energy would grow less intense, the solar panels used on other Pioneers were ruled out and nuclear generators were brought in. Its nine-foot antenna dish was permanently oriented to the Earth's orbit, sending its eight-watt radio signal (about the strength of a night-light) back to Earth. *Pioneer 10* carried 11 scientific instruments to measure magnetic fields, cosmic rays, the solar wind, dust particles, hydrogen abundance and radio waves.

About six weeks before *Pioneer 10* was scheduled for its historic Jupiter flyby, United Press International warned the world of *Pioneer*

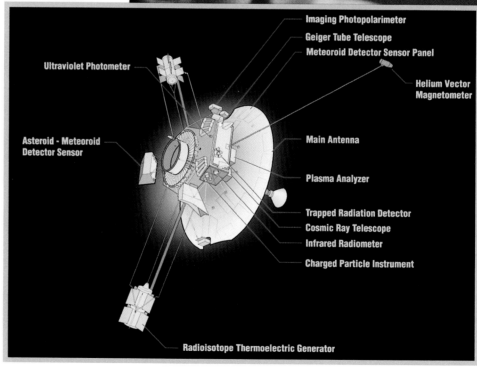

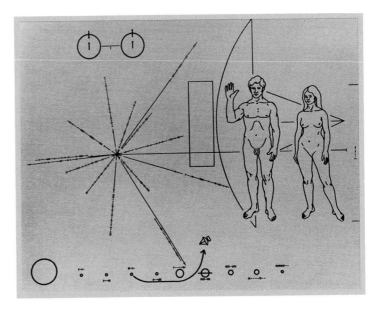

> "*Pioneer 10* opened up a whole new ballgame in the planetary exploration program."
>
> —*Dr. Noel W. Hinners, NASA administrator*

Pioneer 10's instruments included an asteriod detector (opposite) that helped the craft negotiate the belt of debris it traversed on the way to Jupiter; Pioneer project manager Charles Hall (left, gesturing) held regular meetings on the mission's status; *Pioneer*'s plaque (above) showed the sun at bottom left, the planets and the craft's path from Earth past Jupiter.

10's imminent "maiming" by Jupiter's radiation fields. NASA was all too aware of the possibility that *Pioneer 10* could be crippled, and for this reason it had built the craft as cheaply as possible—a fact that was impressed upon Congress. Pioneer's engineers and scientists held their breath as it reached periapsis on December 3, 1973—the closest it would come to Jupiter—a mere 81,000 miles from the planet's cloud tops. A day later, Robert Kraemer, NASA's director of planetary programs, informed the world that *Pioneer 10* had come through with flying colors. "We sent Pioneer to tickle the dragon's tail, and it very much felt the hot breath of radiation from the dragon, and amazingly enough, it survived," he said. "We could hardly have played the game any tighter and come through. Some sensors were 99 percent saturated with radiation before the danger eased off."

Pioneer 10's scientific contributions were immense. It provided the first closeups of Jupiter's surface, including the "Great Red Spot" (bigger in circumference than Earth) and the magnificent gold, white, gray, red, bronze and brown striations of the planet's turbulent clouds. Scientists were able to take accurate measurements of Jupiter's four planet-sized moons: Ganymede, Io, Europa and Callisto. During *Pioneer 10*'s flyby the vessel used Jupiter's gravity to slingshot itself for a course leading out of the solar system at a rate of 270 million miles per year.

Shortly after No. 10's penetration of the asteroid belt, NASA launched *Pioneer 11*, a nearly identical sister craft that also headed for Jupiter but with a great deal more knowledge about the asteroid debris and radiation awaiting it. *Pioneer 11*'s flyby achieved an amazing periapsis only 26,000 miles above Jupiter's cloud tops. After sending back closeups even more stunning than its predecessor's, *Pioneer 11* journeyed on to photograph Saturn before heading off, like its sister, into the interstellar void.

Mission analyst Dave Lozier (above) oversaw the computer that processed data from *Pioneer 10*; an artist's rendering showed the craft against deep space (right); *Pioneer 10*'s images revealed Jupiter's Great Red Spot and striated clouds (below).

Aftermath

Pioneer 10 has had an amazing post-Jupiter career spanning nearly three decades. "We call it an eternal spacecraft" says Richard Fimmel, NASA Pioneer project manager. In June 1983, *Pioneer 10* became the first man-made object to pass beyond Pluto and leave the solar system. Now some seven billion miles from the sun, it is the most remote object ever launched.

In 1997, 25 yearsafter *Pioneer 10*'s launch, NASA held a silver anniversary conference commemorating its voyage. Though NASA's deep space network was still able to pick up *Pioneer*'s ever fainter signal, which by then was diluted from its original eight-watt strength to a mere 4 billionth of a trillionth of a watt, routine tracking was officially ceased. An indication of the enormous distance Pioneer has traveled can be found in the radio signal, which now takes over nine hours to reach Earth, compared to 44 minutes during the 1973 flyby.

The next milepost of *Pioneer 10*'s space odyssey will be the heliopause, the boundary where the effects of the solar wind, the streams of particles hurtling from the sun, dwindle to nothing.

ALL IN THE FAMILY

The year was 1971. America was in turmoil. People were taking sides on everything from school busing to capital punishment to feminism to President Richard Nixon's Vietnam policy. Out of this chaos came a man whose conservative politics, backward ideology and utter disdain for those different from himself helped the country confront and even laugh about its problems. The man's name was Archie Bunker and his pulpit was a weekly television program called *All in the Family*.

Based on the popular and controversial British series *Till Death Us Do Part*, *All in the Family* was developed by veteran writer-producer Norman Lear and his partner, director Alan "Bud" Yorkin. They produced a pilot for ABC originally titled *Those Were the Days* with character actor Carroll O'Connor as Archie, the blustery, bigoted patriarch of the Bunker family. Jean Stapleton, a stage actress, played Archie's kind and oft-confused wife, Edith. After viewing two versions of the pilot ABC remained lukewarm on the show and let its option lapse. CBS executives, impressed by the show's intelligence and willing to take a chance on its controversial content, picked up the series.

Set in Corona, a blue-collar section of Queens, the retitled *All in the Family* premiered on CBS on January 12, 1971. Two significant additions to the cast were Sally Struthers as Archie and Edith's feminist daughter, Gloria, and Rob Reiner as her ultraliberal husband, Mike Stivic. The young couple lived with the Bunkers, and Mike, a full-time student, was constantly at odds with Archie. Mike's opinions, more often than not, lead Archie to label him "pinko," "commie" or, Archie's personal favorite, "meathead." Because of its provocative nature, the first show was preceded

The Bunker household revolved around Archie (left, with cigar), who sang the show's theme song with Edith (above).

"All in the Family" © *CPT Holdings, Inc.*

57

by the announcement, "The program you are about to see is *All in the Family*. It seeks to throw a humorous spotlight on our frailties, prejudices and concerns. By making them a source of laughter we hope to show—in a mature fashion—just how absurd they are."

The debut episode of *All in the Family* was the first sitcom videotaped before a live audience. The program placed only 54th in the weekly Nielsen ratings but its adult topics, edgy dialogue and humor quickly attracted a larger audience. By summer of that year, the show was No. 1. The

Norman Lear (inset, on the set) received an award from the American Civil Liberties Union in 1973 for his "breakthrough" show; **the family played out its argumentaitve style of togetherness in the dining room (top) and at the breakfast table (opposite).**

"Stifle yourself!"

—ARCHIE BUNKER to Edith, repeatedly

series, which dealt with such taboo issues as homosexuality, abortion, rape and menopause, reigned atop the Nielsen ratings for an amazing five years. In 1972 over 50 million people reportedly watched the show regularly—an astonishing audience for a weekly series. America apparently found the Bunker household a refreshing change from the saccharine sitcoms of the '50s and '60s.

Still, some were offended by the racist words like "spic," "hebe" and "spade" that regularly spewed from Archie's mouth; most realized that much of the time the joke was on him. As O'Con-

nor explained his character, "Archie's dilemma is coping with a world that is changing in front of him.... But he won't get to the root of the problem because the root of the problem is himself, and he doesn't know it."

During its run from 1971 to 1979, *All in the Family* presented its audience with an array of colorful characters and situations. Among the participants were Edith's cousin Maude (Bea Arthur), whose Democratic leanings and headstrong personality made for interesting visits with the Bunkers; Sammy Davis Jr., whose hilarious

Gloria and Mike lost a baby before Joey's birth in 1975 (near right); Sammy Davis Jr. (below, right) gave Archie a kiss and a pendant with the motto, "Peace, Love and Sammy"; although animosity reigned between Archie and his neighbor George Jefferson, Edith and Louise Jefferson were good friends (opposite).

guest appearance ended with a shocked Archie surprised to endure a kiss from the star while their picture was snapped; and Frank and Irene Lorenzo (Vincent Gardenia and Betty Garrett), neighbors whose domestic roles flouted tradition—he cooked and cleaned while she operated a forklift and was handy at fixing things. But perhaps the most famous supporting characters on the show were the Bunkers' African-American neighbors, the Jeffersons. When the Jeffersons moved next door to the Bunkers during the first season it hit Archie—figuratively and literally—right where he lived. Louise Jefferson and her son Lionel (Isabel Sanford and Mike Evans) became friends with Edith, Mike and Gloria and did their best to put up with Archie; Louise's husband George and his brother Henry (Sherman Hemsley and Mel Stewart) provided a perfect mirror to Archie by being almost as bigoted as he, but from the other side of the racial divide. Particularly hilarious were the ironic moments when Archie and George, who so clearly despised each other, would find themselves agreeing on their mutual antipathy for a particular ethnic group.

At the conclusion of the 1977-78 season both Rob Reiner and Sally Struthers left the series to pursue other ventures. Soon thereafter Jean Stapleton departed as well and *All in the Family*, as we knew it, was no more. In its eight-year run, *All in the Family* radically reshaped the boundaries of TV comedy. By pointing out our shortcomings and making light of our differences, *All in the Family* made us laugh and, in the process, made us think.

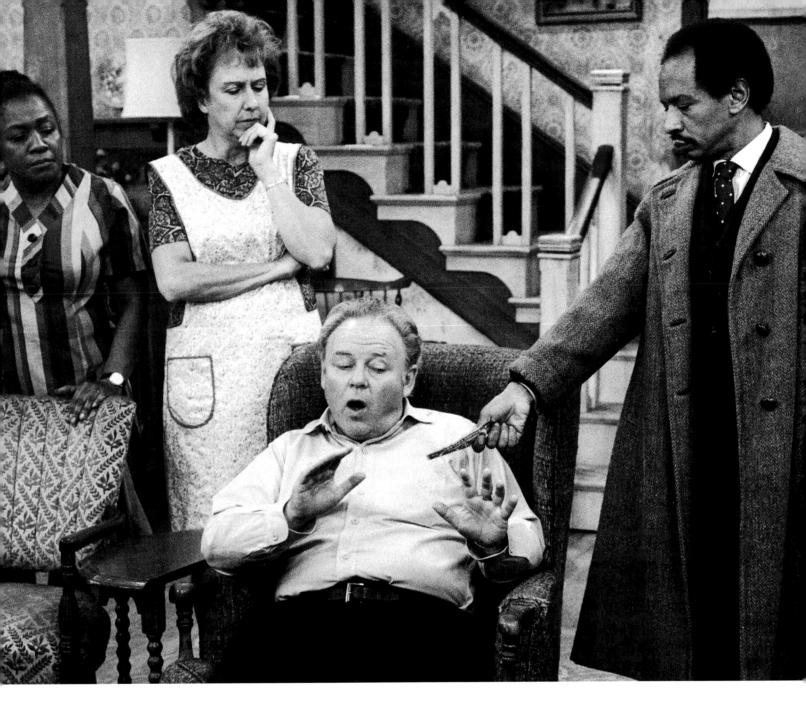

Aftermath

At the beginning of the 1979-80 season, *All in the Family* was renamed *Archie Bunker's Place* after Archie's new venture, a bar where much of the show's action took place. The next season began with Archie grieving over Edith, who had died from a stroke. The final episode was aired in 1983 and marked the end of the "Archie" era.

During its eight-year run, *All in the Family* won 19 Emmy awards, and its influence continues to this day. Direct spin-offs such as *The Jeffersons* and *Maude* continued the tradition of utilizing "hot-button" issues in their story lines while more distant relatives like *Soap, Cheers* and *Seinfeld*, which regularly featured risqué humor, all owe a large debt to the trailblazing *All in the Family*.

PITTSBURGH STEELERS

They waited a long time for a winning football team in Pittsburgh, but it was worth the wait. Founded in 1933 by a generous Steel City Irishman named Art Rooney, the Pittsburgh Steelers enjoyed only eight winning seasons in their first 39 years. During that span Pittsburgh did not win a single playoff game and made several blunders in the front office, such as releasing a quarterback named Johnny Unitas in 1955. Theirs was a stolid, comically predictable style of football. In the early '50s Pittsburgh fans chanted "Hi diddle diddle, Rogel up the middle," in anticipation of the team's first play from scrimmage, which invariably turned out to be a handoff to running back Fran Rogel.

All that changed with the dawn of the 1970s, when the Steelers established one of pro football's greatest dynasties—and two fateful events precipitated the change. The first was a coin toss. The Chicago Bears called heads, and when the coin showed tails, the Steelers won the right to the first pick of the 1970 NFL draft. They chose a quarterback from Louisiana named Terry Bradshaw, who would be involved in the franchise's second destiny-shaping event, known in Steelers scripture as the Immaculate Reception.

One of the strangest plays in NFL history, it happened on December 23, 1972, when the young quarterback, facing fourth down on the Pittsburgh 40-yard line, threw a desperation pass over the middle toward running back Frenchy Fuqua. The Steelers trailed the Oakland Raiders 7–6 with 22 seconds remaining in their AFC playoff game. Thirty-nine years of playoff futility, it seemed, would stretch into 40. But Bradshaw's pass deflected off defender Jack Tatum's shoulder and ricocheted eight yards back toward the line of scrimmage, where it was plucked out of the air, inches from the Astroturf, by Pittsburgh rookie running back Franco Harris.

Whether he was asking the crowd for quiet (left) or handing off to Harris (above), Bradshaw was the Steelers' engine.

After years of futility, beloved Steelers owner Art Rooney (above) had a winning team; with Noll (left) as the guiding light on the bench and Harris (right) as the sparkplug on the field, the Steelers won four Super Bowls in six seasons.

Harris ran 42 yards for the game-winning touchdown. "That play," said Steelers head coach Chuck Noll, "was a sign that this was a team of destiny."

Noll was surely right, but Pittsburgh's destiny would be delayed until 1974, when they again improved themselves through the draft with a sensational haul that included wide receiver Lynn Swann, fearsome linebacker Jack Lambert, John Stallworth, Swann's receiving mate, and future Hall of Fame center Mike Webster. The '74 Steelers went 10–3–1 and dispatched the Buffalo Bills and the Oakland Raiders in the playoffs to reach their first Super Bowl. All of the pieces of

the Steelers dynasty were in place—in addition to the aforementioned stars, the Steelers had future Hall of Fame linebacker Jack Ham, defensive tackle "Mean" Joe Greene, perhaps the best ever at his position, and defensive back Mel Blount, another of the seven Steelers who would reach the Hall. But no one seemed to recognize it at the time: The Minnesota Vikings were installed as favorites in Super Bowl IX. The Steel Curtain defense fell on them, however, and Pittsburgh, after 42 years of loyal support, finally had its champion. The Steelers won 16–6.

The Steel City clasped its beloved team even tighter

> **"What we had was an undeniable hatred of losing. We despised losing! Woe be to the fool who came into our stadium on Sunday. We had the fangs and the blood and the slobber! We loved it, Jack!"**
>
> —*TERRY BRADSHAW, Pittsburgh Steelers quarterback*

to its bosom now. "The fans," said Webster, "with their motor homes and kielbasa, they were the most important thing." Said longtime Pittsburgh broadcaster and writer Myron Cope, "Steelers fans are unlike any other football following. Those teams of the '70s—they could have played a game in Zanzibar, and there'd be 200 fans waiting for them at the hotel when they arrived."

Those fans surely would have been happy with the one Super Bowl triumph, but their beloved Steelers were far from done. After a 12–2 season in '75, Pittsburgh again reached the Super Bowl, where they faced the Dallas Cowboys. The best of

the 10 Super Bowls to date ensued as game-MVP Swann turned the tide with an acrobatic 64-yard touchdown reception that remains in the canon of NFL highlights. The Steelers won, 21–17.

Pittsburgh's most impressive stretch during its '70s dynasty came, ironically, in 1976, a year they failed to reach the Super Bowl. They began the season without Bradshaw, who was hurt, and went 1–4. When Bradshaw returned, the offense righted itself and the defense became unbeatable. Over the remaining nine games, all victories, the Steeler D pitched five shutouts and yielded a paltry 28 points.

The wheels came off in the AFC title game, however, as Pittsburgh, playing without injured running backs Harris and Rocky Bleier, lost to Oakland, 24–7. The Steelers returned to the height of their considerable powers in 1978. That season's 14–2 team is rated by many as the best in NFL history. After routing two playoff opponents, Pittsburgh was back in the big one, and their 35–31 victory over Dallas was not as close as the score would suggest. Bradshaw was named MVP of Super Bowl XIII, after a year in which he won the passing title and was named NFL Player of the Year. Following the victory, their third title in five years, Coach Noll gathered his players round and told them, "This team hasn't peaked yet."

"Way to put the pressure on, Coach," cracked Webster, but it didn't matter. The next year Pittsburgh won its fourth Super Bowl, beating the Los Angeles Rams, 31–19.

The legendary Steel Curtain defense was anchored by, among other talented players, L. C. Greenwood (top, No. 68), Greene (No. 75) and the snarling Lambert (above); one all-time Steeler highlight was an acrobatic catch by Swann over Dallas defender Mark Washington in Super Bowl X (right).

Aftermath

A combination of advancing age and injuries brought the Steelers dynasty to an abrupt close in 1980. The team went 9–7 that year and missed the playoffs. Pittsburgh would rise again in '83, as Bradshaw overcame an injured elbow to lead the Steelers to a 10–6 record and a division title. But waiting in the first round of the playoffs were the eventual Super Bowl champion L.A. Raiders, who prevailed 38–10. Bradshaw retired after that season and was inducted into the Hall of Fame in 1989.

With Mark Malone calling the signals, the Steelers won their division in '84 with a 9–7 record and made it to the AFC title game, in which they lost to the Miami Dolphins, 45–28. The lean years of the late '80s led to coach Chuck Noll's retirement in 1991, after 22 years with the club. Bill Cowher, a native of Pittsburgh, took over and with Neil O'Donnell at quarterback, the Steelers returned to the Super Bowl after the '95 season. O'Donnell threw three interceptions in a 27–17 loss to Dallas.

WOMEN'S RIGHTS MOVEMENT

On an April morning in 1959, I heard a mother of four, having coffee with four other mothers in a suburban development 15 miles from New York, say in a tone of quiet desperation, "the problem." And the others knew, without words, that she was not talking about a problem with her husband, or her children, or her home. Suddenly they realized they all shared the same problem, the problem that has no name.

Many more women than the five Betty Friedan overheard that April morning shared the problem that she identified in her book *The Feminine Mystique*, published in 1963. In the book she indicted the marketers, educators, psychologists and sociologists whose work perpetuated the stifling notion that women ought to find fulfillment not through accomplishments outside the home but rather through nurturing their families. Women responded to Friedan's analysis by the thousands, flooding her mailbox with letters and making her book the best-selling nonfiction paperback of 1964. Of course, the uneasiness and dissatisfaction that Friedan described was experienced primarily by well-educated, married, middle-class white women. For many other American women—working-class women, women of color, single women—working was an economic necessity; fulfillment was not at issue. Nevertheless, the idea that women belonged in the home and not in the working world hurt all working women, who enjoyed fewer job opportunities and were paid less than men. Confined largely to clerical and service jobs, white women in 1960 earned only 60 cents for every dollar earned by white men, down from 63.9 cents to a dollar in 1955.

In the same year *The Feminine Mystique* was

Women took to the streets (left) to voice their views on critical issues such as the Equal Rights Amendment (above).

I am now a feminist. I am infused with pride—in my sisters, in myself, in my womanhood."

—SOPHY BURNHAM, a journalist who had thought of feminists as "a lunatic fringe" before she researched and wrote about the movement, in September 1970

Congresswoman Bella Abzug (above, left) and *Ms.* magazine editor Gloria Steinem (above, right) were prominent figures in the women's movement, along with Betty Friedan (right); 100,000 people marched in a pro-ERA demonstration in Washington, D.C. in July 1978 (opposite).

published, the Presidential Commission on the Status of Women, chaired by Eleanor Roosevelt, issued a report that painstakingly described the social, economic and legal discrimination confronted by women of all classes. The commission drew together a network of female lawyers, academics, union leaders and other professionals. At the same time, thousands of ordinary women were honing their organizational skills working in the civil rights and New Left movements with groups such as the Student Nonviolent Coordinating Committee (SNCC) and Students for a Democratic Society (SDS). Almost all of the leaders were male, and many were frankly uninterested in women's issues. Prominent activist Stokely Carmichael said, "The only position for women in SNCC is prone."

In reaction to such attitudes, women formed their own organizations. The best-known of the new groups was the National Organization for Women, founded in 1966 by Friedan and several other delegates to the third National Conference of State Commissions on the Status of Women. NOW declared that it would "take action to bring women into full participation in the mainstream of American society now, assuming all the privileges and responsibilities thereof in truly equal partnership with men."

By 1970 this "second wave" of American feminism (the first wave culminated in 1920 with the passage of the Nineteenth Amendment granting women the right to vote) had won both visibility and credibility. When NOW called for a Women's Strike for Equality on August 26, 1970, to celebrate the 50th anniversary of the passage of the Nineteenth Amendment, thousands of women marched and demonstrated in cities across the nation and attracted thousands more to their cause. Several legal victories soon followed. In 1972, five decades after it was first debated, Congress passed the Equal Rights Amendment, which stated that "men and women shall have equal rights throughout the United States and every place subject to its jurisdiction." By the end of the year, 22 states had ratified the ERA.

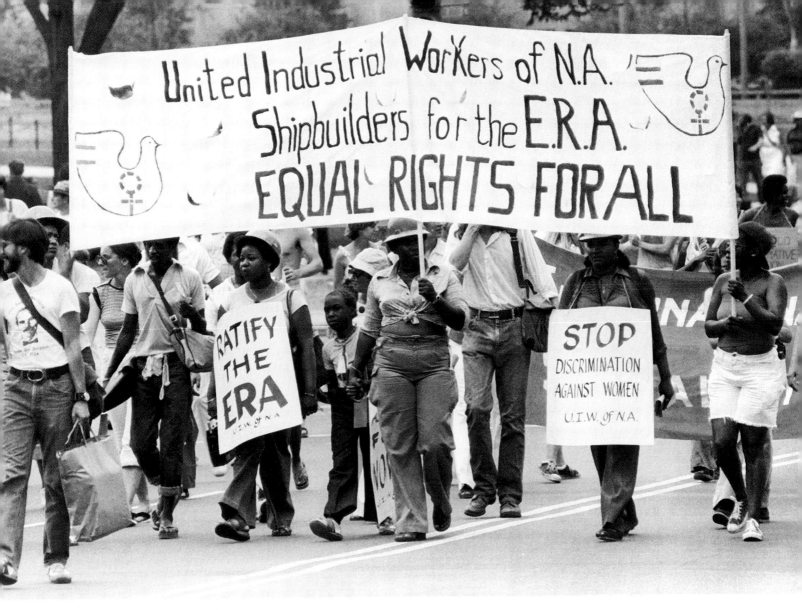

That year also saw the passage of the Higher Education Act, which legislated in Title IX that "No person in the United States shall, on the basis of sex, be excluded from participation in, be denied the benefits of, or be subjected to discrimination under any education program or activity receiving federal financial assistance." This law made possible the explosive growth of female participation in college athletics. And in 1973 the Supreme Court's ruling in *Roe v. Wade* upheld the right to abortion.

At the grass-roots level, women founded rape crisis centers and hotlines, women's health clinics, shelters for battered women, childcare centers, newspapers and journals. Organizations such as Nine-to-Five in Boston and Women Employed in

Chicago protested assigning housewifely chores to female office workers. Women Employed staged a demonstration on February 3, 1977, that won back the job of Iris Rivera, a legal secretary who had been fired because she refused to make coffee, stating that "One, I don't drink coffee. Two, it's not listed as one of my job duties, and three, ordering the secretaries to fix the coffee is carrying the role of homemaker too far." In small consciousness-raising groups women shared and analyzed their experiences to discover that "the personal is political." That proposition, writes poet and social critic Katha Pollitt, "was a way of saying that what looked like individual experiences, with little social resonance and certainly no polit-

Harvard graduates advertised their feminism at the 1971 commencement (right); two of the hardest fought and most polarizing issues of the decade were the Equal Rights Amendment, passed by Congress and approved by 35 states (above), and abortion rights (opposite).

ical importance—rape, street harassment, you doing the vacuuming while your husband reads the paper—were part of a general pattern of male domination and female subordination."

By the end of the decade, 52 percent of all adult women were working outside the home, and increasingly they were taking their place in fields long dominated by men. In 1980, for instance, 23 percent of medical school graduates and 28.5 percent of law school graduates were women, compared to only 8.4 and 5.4 percent, respectively, in 1970. However slowly, tradition was yielding to feminism's second wave.

Aftermath

In 1982 the deadline for ratifying the ERA ran out, and the amendment was defeated, falling shy by three of the 38 states needed. According to Susan Faludi's bestseller, *Backlash*, published in 1991, such disappointment was characteristic of a decade in which the conservatism of the Reagan administration held sway, and the mass media spoke of "the death of feminism." The work of second-wave feminists to redefine women's roles and needs could not be undone, however, and women's status continued to grow. In 1999 a record number of women—56—were serving in Congress, women were earning about 75 percent as much as men and 14 percent of the members of the armed forces were women.

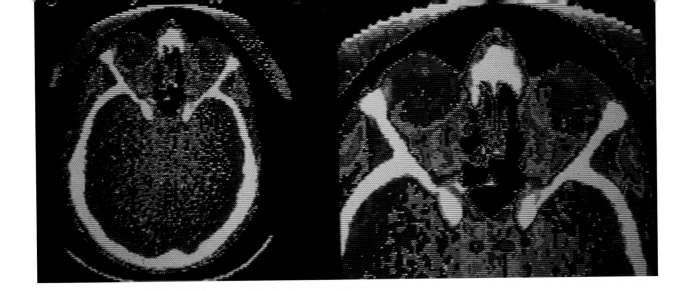

MEDICAL IMAGING

In the 1970s doctors, physicists and engineers found new ways to use x-rays, sound waves and magnetic fields to see the interior of the living body. A new generation of computers that worked faster and had bigger memories was essential to these new technologies—computed tomography, ultrasound and magnetic resonance imaging. Until these powerful computers entered the picture, even the most futuristic dreamer could make little headway toward developing the devices and procedures that created a revolution in diagnosing disease.

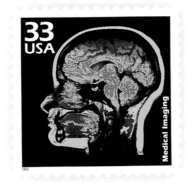

The CT (short for computed tomography) scanner uses x-rays in a very different way from a conventional x-ray machine, which works somewhat like a camera, taking snapshots of the body's interior on photographic film. A CT image is assembled bit by bit as an x-ray tube rotates around the patient, sending a narrow x-ray beam from many different angles through the body to detectors opposite the tube. The amount of radiation that reaches a detector depends on what kind of tissue it has passed through—bone, for instance, absorbs x-rays in large quantities, while softer tissues absorb less. Each detector emits a flash of light indicating how much radiation it receives, and a computer measures the light, then stores its location and magnitude. When the scanning process is complete, the computer constructs an anatomical image of a cross section, or slice, through the body and displays it on a screen. Along with organs and bones, tumors, infections, hemorrhages and other abnormalities show up on a scan, like the seeds and ribs on the surface of a halved tomato.

The first CT machine went on the market in 1972. Used only for scans of the head, the machine was immediately successful as a diagnostic tool. Physicians had been dreaming of a sharp view of a living, functioning brain ever since Wilhelm Roentgen's discovery of x-rays in 1895. Psychiatrists quickly took advantage of CT scans to examine the brains of the mentally ill for anatomical abnormali-

The CT machine (left) painlessly opened the body to view, producing images like those of the brain shown above.

ties. In people suffering from schizophrenia, scans revealed that the brain's cavities, or ventricals, were often enlarged, and the furrows on the convoluted surface of the cerebral cortex, where higher functions like cognition and speech take place, were wider than normal.

With the advent of the head scanner, a rush was soon on to design a machine that could scan any part of the body, from head to toe. Head scans took about four minutes to make, but a machine that could scan the entire body would have to do its work

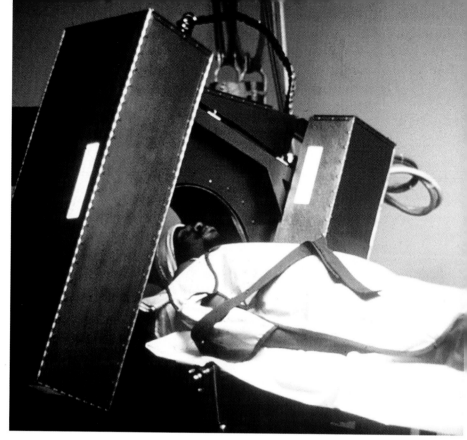

in the time that a patient could hold his or her breath; otherwise, the movement of breathing would distort the image. By 1975, whole-body scanners costing about $500,000 were in use. They drastically reduced the need for risky, expensive and painful exploratory surgery and quickly became essential equipment for radiologists and emergency rooms.

Pregnant women and their fetuses were basically off limits for diagnosis via x-rays, since obstetricians knew that prenatal exposure could lead to cancer. Fortunately, ultrasound offered an alternative for taking a baby's first picture. The medical profession borrowed sonar technology, which had evolved during World War II to detect enemy submarines by aiming very high-frequency, inaudible sound waves under water and picking up the echoes when they bounced off submerged

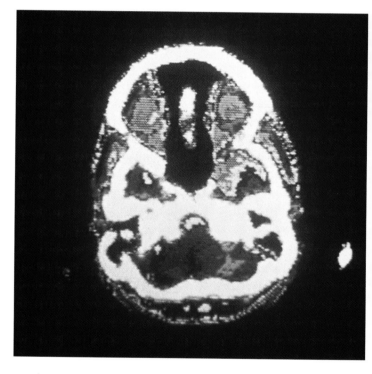

"There is a beauty and an intuitive appeal to the brain-scanning methods, especially the high-resolution MRI pictures...."

—*KAY REDFIELD JAMISON, psychologist*

76

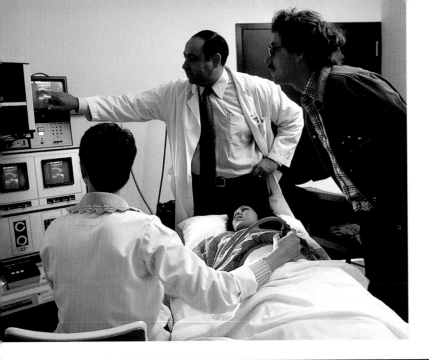

objects. To capture a fetus's image, a small probe called a transducer was invented that, when placed on the mother's abdomen, generates sound and receives the echoes from the fetus. Depending on their density, different tissues have distinctive echoes, which are translated by a computer into electronic signals and displayed on a television screen in a range of subtle grays.

By the end of the 1970s, nearly half of all pregnancies in the U.S. were being monitored by ultrasound to determine a fetus's age, to see whether the mother was carrying more than one baby or to detect birth defects or abnormalities of the placenta. The process also made amniocentesis safer. Before ultrasound, one specialist explained, inserting a needle into the amniotic sac to extract a sample of fetal cells was risky: "There was always the chance of jabbing it into some vital area. Now you can see where the head, heart, and umbilical cord are."

Besides watching over the unborn child, ultrasound probed for blocked bile ducts and prostate trouble and, by decade's end, was so sophisticated that a cardiologist could watch the motion of a beating heart in real time.

As the '70s came to a close, physicians were eagerly awaiting the first magnetic resonance imaging (MRI) machines to go on the market. The process employs a giant tube-shaped superconducting magnet and radio signals from the scanner to search out differences in water content in the body's tissues. A computer uses the information gathered by the scanner's

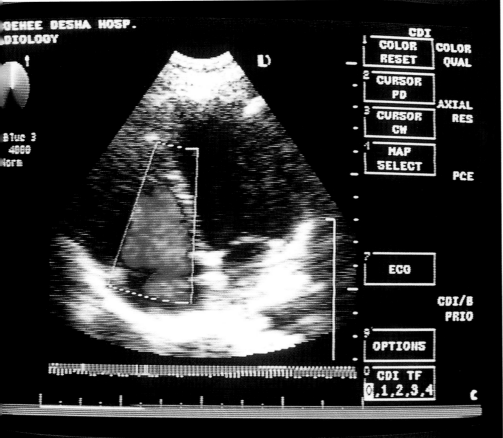

During an ultrasound examination a physician discussed the monitor's display (top); less expensive than CT, ultrasound technology was affordable even for small medical centers like the rural hospital at which the image above was made; American physician Robert Ledley's 1974 CT machine (opposite, above) was the first that could image the entire body; his machine made the cross-sectional image of the head shown opposite, below.

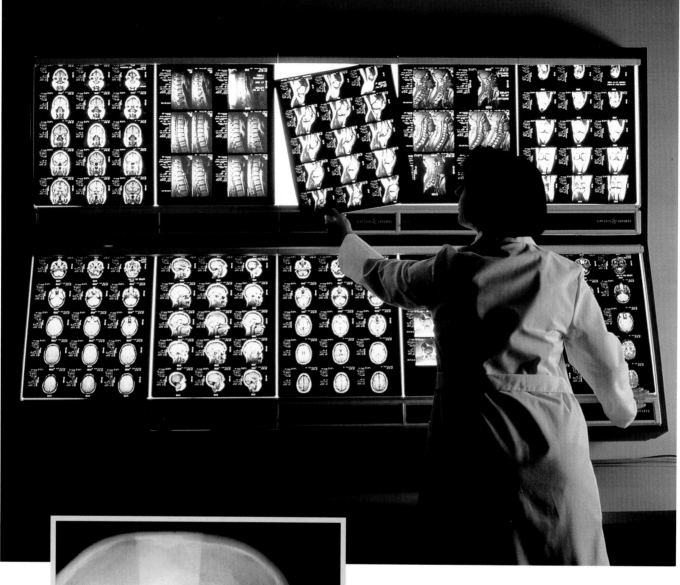

CT scans (above) aided the diagnosis of brain tumors, cancers and other disorders difficult or impossible to see in conventional x-ray images (left); giving a patient a solution that absorbs x-rays made the urinary tract appear bluish and stand out clearly in the x-ray (right).

antenna to map the outlines of the tissues and display the image on a screen. Like a CT scan, each MRI scan shows a beautifully detailed slice through the body, but with none of the known risks posed by x-rays. No one could actually prove that the powerful magnetic field was harmless to patients, but since human beings spend their lives on a giant magnet—the earth—researchers and physicians plunged optimistically into the brave new world of MRI.

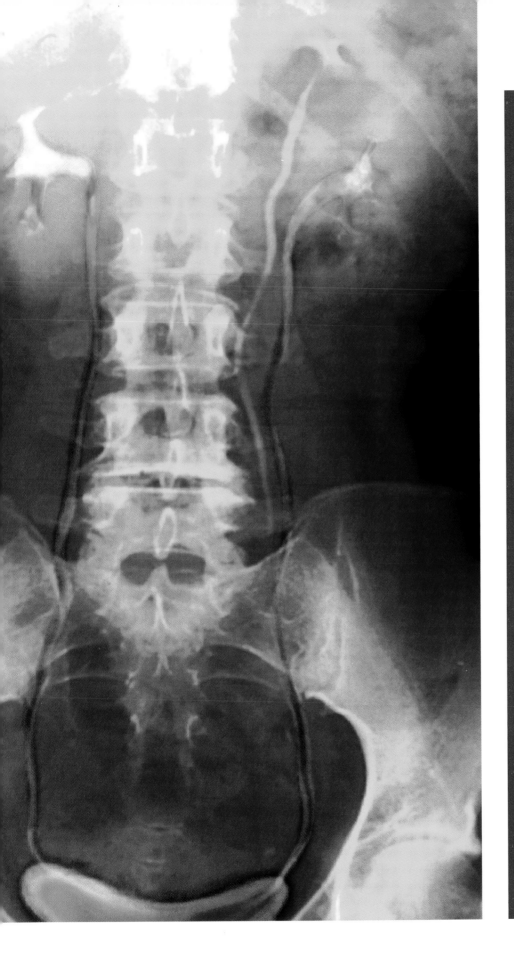

Aftermath

CT technology was less than a decade old when it played a critical role in the trial of John Hinckley, the man who shot President Ronald Reagan and his press secretary, James Brady, in 1981 in a bizarre attempt to impress actress Jodie Foster. To bolster psychiatric testimony that he was schizophrenic at the time of the shooting and shouldn't be held criminally responsible, Hinckley's lawyers presented a CT scan showing abnormalities in his brain. It was the first time a CT scan was accepted as evidence in a U.S. court, and it was evidently persuasive. The jury found Hinckley legally insane, and he was confined in a mental hospital in Washington, D.C.

At century's end, state-of-the-art ultrasound, CTs and MRIs are making the body amazingly transparent. Physicians diagnose once elusive diseases such as multiple sclerosis and record the changes in brain anatomy in patients suffering from Alzheimer's disease and posttraumatic stress disorder. Surgeons routinely rely on CT and MRI scans when they plan operations. Operations can even be performed inside a specialized MRI machine that displays closeup images of the site the surgeon is working on (with nonmagnetic tools) in almost real time.

SMILEY FACE

In the '40s it was "Kilroy Was Here." Then came "I Like Ike" in the '50s, followed by "Make Love, Not War" in the '60s. Each of these slogans was right for its decade and, one after another, each caught on with the public and won a permanent place in the American collective consciousness. Then came the '70s. Once again, a decade-distinctive catch phrase emerged, but this time it was paired with a drawing worthy of a kindergartner with a steady hand. For better or worse, what took America by storm was a bright yellow disk, with two dots for eyes, an arc for a mouth and the accompanying injunction to "Have a Nice Day." Where the name came from no one knows, but this character came to be known everywhere as "Smiley Face."

Smiley Face made its appearance in the 1960s as one of the ubiquitous buttons that people sported in those years, usually to make a statement about their political persuasion. It is uncertain who actually designed the smiling yellow icon, although many have taken credit. A New York radio station, a Seattle ad agency, a freelance commercial artist from Massachusetts and a French entrepreneur are among those who claim the famous face as their own creation. Whatever its origin, Smiley Face took on a life of its own in the 1970s and was soon on its way to becoming a pop icon.

In the early '70s N. G. Slater, a New York-based button manufacturer, and Traffic Stoppers, a Philadelphia company, were selling millions of Smiley Face-emblazoned products to novelty shops and discount stores across the country. The image cropped up on blue jeans, pillowcases, notepads, T-shirts and key chains. Traffic Stoppers was inspired to add the words "Have a Happy Day" to their Smiley products. The sentence eventually evolved into "Have a Nice Day" and has been inextricably connected to Smiley ever since.

Smiley Faces embellished everything from alarm clocks and tape dispensers (left) to a hillside in England (above).

Smiley Face took part in a women's liberation march in New York City on August 25, 1971 (left) and beamed skyward from an Arizona arena rooftop (above); the multihued Smileys on the cocktail shaker at right departed from the norm in color.

Despite its seeming vacuousness, Smiley Face was not just an icon for the young, happy and mindless. It was soon appropriated for more high-profile and serious purposes than decorating jeans and home furnishings. In 1972, the Democratic presidential candidate, George McGovern, paired Smiley with an upbeat daisy design on his campaign bumper stickers. Alas, this dynamic combination was not enough to defeat the incumbent, Richard Nixon.

Smiley Face also made its way onto schoolwork in sticker form or drawn by hand, placed there by teachers to give students praise for work well done. Conversely, many of those teachers would put a frowning Smiley on tests and papers they thought were not up to par. In a bit of overkill, many kids and even some adults started dotting their "i"s with Smiley Faces. On the culinary side, birthday cakes with sunny yellow icing and the trademark features were popular at kid's parties.

At the height of its popularity, the Smiley Face appealed to the carriage trade as well as to children. The exclusive jeweler Cartier offered Smiley pins in precious metals, and Bergdorf Goodman, a department store on New York's Fifth Avenue, sold 14-karat gold cigarette

Aftermath

Although its popularity waned in the late '70s, the Smiley Face by no means disappeared. It resurfaced repeatedly during the 1980s and '90s.

In the 1994 Academy Award-winning movie *Forrest Gump*, Tom Hanks played the unwitting hero, Forrest, who was present at many historical events of the '50s, '60s and '70s. In the '70s segment Forrest is credited with creating the Smiley Face when he dries his mud-caked face with a yellow T-shirt and exclaims, "Have a nice day!"

In 1998 Massachusetts freelance artist Harvey Ball—who claims to have created Smiley Face in 1963 for an insurance company campaign developed by Joy P. Young (at left, with Ball)—filed a trademark infringement suit against Frenchman Franklin Loufrani, who trademarked the rights to Smiley in much of the world in the '70s. "He's a creep," Ball said when asked about Loufrani. Certainly, unSmiley-like language.

"Have a Nice Day."
—*Smiley Face*

lighters, pillows and other items bearing the cheery visage.

It was probably inevitable that Smiley Face's relentless cheerfulness would get on some people's nerves and prompt them to take revenge by creating cynical new versions of the icon. Novelty companies took the baton and ran with it, altering the yellow face to make it look intoxicated, for instance, or angry. Yet other Smileys appeared with new tag phrases. Inevitably, some of the second-generation Smileys were obscene. One curious substitution for "Have a Nice Day" was "Don't Eat Yellow Snow."

Like many pop icons and fads before it, the sunshiny Smiley Face rode off into the sunset. In what author Tom Wolfe called "the 'Me' decade" Smiley

Face could be viewed as the antithesis of selfishness and narcissism.

Whether loved or hated, the yellow symbol made its mark both literally and figuratively, as those who wore it on a pin or patch or shirt seemed either exceptionally friendly and approachable or vacuous and inane, depending on your point of view.

While the Smiley Face may not have exactly defined or represented the '70s as symbols of previous generations had, it did succeed on a small scale in helping America through another trying decade. The constant bombardment of smiling yellow faces helped Americans forget, if only for a moment, such problems as the continuing strife over Vietnam, Watergate, the gas shortage and, yes, even disco.

FASHION IN THE '70S

"Fashion as a dictatorship of the elite is dead!" That assertion concerning 1970s fashion was made by *Cheap Chic*, a popular guide of the day that offered "hundreds of money-saving hints to create your own great look." Reflecting the essence of the '70s attitude toward fashion, the guide preached the democratization of dressing—urging its readers to freely sample the gaudy array of fashion choices: wide-lapelled polyester leisure suits, broad, flashy ties, bell-bottomed pants, Afghan coats, Indian scarves, platform shoes, "Annie Hall" gender-bending hats and ties for women, feminist anti-fashion, retro '50s leather jackets, disco spandex, punk zippers and chains and designer jeans.

The critical break with "fashion fascism" came in 1970. For the fall season, Paris designers decreed a radical plunge in hemlines from the reigning miniskirt to the calf-length "midi," and manufacturers across the Atlantic meekly obeyed.

Outraged, millions of American women simply refused to buy the new clothes. Fashion critic Mary Peacock recalled the effects of the boycott in *Rolling Stone: The '70s*: "The politics of 'midi' permanently changed the way fashion design worked. Stores with floors full of a truly disastrous style clarified to women the fact that fashion was not a democracy. So they voted with their wallets, and from then on the industry started listening to its customers."

Feminism, civil rights, the antiwar movement, environmentalism, gay liberation and hippie antiauthoritarianism were just a few of the causes and ideologies, many of them holdovers from the '60s, that influenced the predominant fashions of the '70s. But whereas the '60s counterculture style signaled certain beliefs, political attitudes and lifestyle choices, '70s offbeat clothing lost its political element and became mainstream, commercialized and deradicalized. Clothes were less of a

Women labeled the calf-length midi "fashion fascism" (left) and wore their miniskirts with platform shoes (above).

statement and more of a "costume"—a way of adopting a new persona or simply a new look.

The '70s fashion "free-for-all" had begun. Vintage and ethnic clothing and accessories were mixed with mass-produced garments to create highly idiosyncratic and ever-changing styles. Men and women complemented their eclectic ensembles with garishly colored and dangerously high platform shoes, but only for a short time; by 1972 they had gone out of style.

Denim was a close second, but polyester reigned supreme over the panoply of fashion choices, proving itself a staple of the decade. The fabric was created from synthetic molecules, melt-spun from terephthalic acid and ethylene glycol, then stitched to create fade-proof and wrinkle-free clothing. Freed from the tyranny of ironing, both sexes snapped up washable double-knit polyester outfits that they wore straight out of the dryer.

At the office, men wore close-fitting long-line jackets with wide lapels, tailored hiphugger pants and gaudy ties. For an evening out, the well-dressed '70s man might put on a frilly lavender eighteenth-century style shirt, a multicolored Indian vest and a pair of dark red velvet jeans tucked into tall black riding boots. For more casual occasions, a double-knit leisure suit, often in baby blue or mint green—sans tie—was a popular choice.

One fashion innovation that women of all sizes, shapes and ages adopted with enthusiasm was the pantsuit. Although some tradition-minded employers banned them at first, pantsuits and more casual pants outfits became common in the workplace, lending efficiency and ease to women's wardrobes. Wrote Peacock, "The most subtle '70s fashion alteration was the rise and triumph of American sportswear: softly tailored jackets, pants and skirts.... Halston, Anne Klein, Calvin Klein, Ralph Lauren and many other designers created simple, dignified

"Everybody wears clown suits these days. Denim jackets and leisure suits. Bellbottoms! Everybody wants to look like a life-style now."

—R. CRUMB,
cartoonist and satirist

Unisex styles blurred gender differences (above), and formfitting clothes and flashy patterns (right) came into favor; the '60s hippie headband went mainstream (near left), while slinky bodysuits and candy-colored coats appeared on fashion runways (opposite).

Seventies fashion ran the gamut from sexy hot pants and peekaboo denims (opposite, right and left) to high-style pantsuits (above) and ensembles (right) to funky knit minidresses (above, right).

clothes that women could wear without making a big production of getting dressed."

Even though it sometimes verged on colorful farce, the costume-ball fashion experimentation of the '70s encouraged people to follow their own instincts. When *Vogue* magazine declared, "There are no rules in the fashion game now," it was confirmation from the highest authority that individual choice and style—no matter how casual or sleek, low-key or bizarre—was here to stay.

Aftermath

Once characterized as "the decade taste forgot," '70s styles returned with a nostalgic fervor in the 1990s. Boutiques were filled with platform shoes, frilled shirts and bellbottom pants, with new upscale incarnations of polyester as the fabric of choice. One advertising executive credited the boom to Generation Xers' TV habits: "They are watching these old shows and are picking up on what the characters are wearing. The beauty is that these kids don't know that there was any baggage to these labels. They are discovering them for the first time." Much as it was the first time around, however, the second '70s fashion craze appeared on the wane by decade's end.

DISCO

The days of disco were days of excess: The beat was heavy, the volume was loud, the sex was liberated and the drugs were abundant. Inhibitions were happily checked at the door, and the gyrating crowd jamming the dance floor went through its funky paces to music that sprang from rhythm and blues. Disco dancing got its start in gay and black nightclubs, was popularized in spots like Studio 54 and Hurrah in Manhattan and immortalized by the 1978 film *Saturday Night Fever* starring John Travolta as Tony Manero, a working-class Brooklyn boy who rules the dance floor at the Odyssey 2001.

Disco lay at the opposite end of the spectrum from the rock and folk music that was emblematic of the 1960s in its call for social awareness. The music pulsed with pleasure and self-indulgence. "You Should Be Dancing" and "Do the Hustle!" were not high-minded calls to action, but club patrons weren't looking for a message. The music was also a departure from the '60s because it was largely producer-driven rather than artist-centered. Musicians were deemphasized in favor of computer-programmed synthesizers and drum machines that manufactured music mainly from the elements of rhythm and blues. With the advent of discos, people frequented clubs featuring prerecorded music instead of a live band, and what mattered was seeing, being seen and dancing.

Sexual themes pervaded the bass drum-driven disco ditties and reinforced the mantra: party, party, party. Donna Summer was christened the Disco Diva for such hits as "Hot Stuff" and "Love to Love You Baby," and Gloria Gaynor's melodramatic scorned-woman hit "I Will Survive" became a disco club anthem. So powerful was the impetus to dance that some young women preferred going to clubs on gay nights to disco-dance without getting propositioned by men. Dance crazes like the Hustle were

Saturday Night Fever star John Travolta (left) and the Village People, famed for "Y.M.C.A."(above), were disco icons.

"**Disco was beautiful because it made the consumer beautiful. The consumer was the star. Disco was about elegance. The consumer was superelegant and that's how I wanted the music. The elegant people wanted to dance to elegant music.**"

—*BARRY WHITE, singer*

spin-offs of hit singles, while others like the Bump germinated on the dance floor.

The most glamorous of all destinations for disco dancers was New York City's Studio 54, which opened in 1977. The club was, according to one observer, "more than a disco. It was a world of fantasy and freedom, where everyone joined in the pulsating ritual of music, dance, ecstasy." A frequent visitor called the club "the center of the universe."

The action at Studio 54 wasn't just dancing. Illegal drug use and sexual antics were common-place in the infamous unisex bathrooms as well as in the basement and even on the dance floor. Every night a giant silver "man-in-the-moon cokehead" mobile descended to the dance floor proffering a cocaine spoon. The scene was dominated by a naive hedonism, without regard for consequences.

Affluent teenagers and young professionals donned their funkiest clothes and lined up at Studio 54 to work up a sweat on the dance floor alongside the "beautiful people"—Liz Taylor, Diana Ross,

Studio 54 co-owner Steve Rubell (above, far left) counted among his regulars (from left to right) Liza Minelli, Bianca Jagger, Andy Warhol and Hal- ston; the balcony of the club gave a bird's-eye view of the dance floor frenzy (right); crowds hoping to get in gathered outside the club at night (inset).

Diana Vreeland, Mikhail Baryshnikov, Betty Ford, Liza Minelli, Margaux Hemingway, and others. Pop artist Andy Warhol, a Studio 54 fixture, would finesse a cover shot for the next issue of his magazine, *Interview*, between songs and hobnobbing. The club was, in the words of Bob Colacello, the executive editor of *Interview*, "as important a New York destination as the Empire State Building."

The hip fashions of the day—glamorous off-the-shoulder gowns, sparkly makeup and see-through blouses—were as much a part of the scene as the dancing and the music. "We want everybody to be fun and good-looking," said Studio 54 co-owner Steve Rubell of his method of deciding who was permitted behind the club's velvet ropes. He rejected any man wearing his collar outside his jacket. "I hate that. And I hate those plaid polyester shirts or those double-knit suits. It looks like *Saturday Night Fever*. We don't want that look."

The look and sound of *Saturday Night Fever*, though, appealed to a large portion of the nation's young adults. By 1978, 37 million people had stormed to 10,000 discos nationwide. Disco accounted for 20 of *Billboard* magazine's Top 100 songs that year, and more than 200 radio stations converted to an all-disco format. Tony Manero wannabes boogied to the *SNF* soundtrack, which was recorded by the disco group the Bee Gees and sold 30 million copies worldwide. The record

Aftermath

The "Kill Disco" movement raged in the late '70s and early 1980s, precipitating the genre's last all-nighter. The disco sound stagnated, and dancers grew bored with the repetitive lyrics and rhythms. A victim of its own wild popularity, disco descended into parody.

One of the last disco albums released was Donna Summer's *Bad Girls* in '79. Summer practically dropped from sight as the decade closed, but she made a comeback in the mid-'80s with the hit "She Works Hard for the Money."

Studio 54 was shuttered in March 1986, and three years later Steve Rubell died of AIDS.

In 1998 a crop of movies, including *The Last Days of Disco* and *54*, paid tribute to the genre. Disco is most often resurrected as feel-good wedding fare or for 1970s theme nights at nightclubs. The music's legacy can be heard in so-called electronica or techno dance music, and echoes of its bass-heavy sound also reverberate in hip-hop.

spawned three number-one hits—"Night Fever," "Stayin' Alive" and "How Deep Is Your Love"—and won the Grammy for Best Album in 1978.

The end of disco was approaching when the Village People recorded "Y.M.C.A." and "Macho Man." In fact, some people blamed the group for turning the music and the lifestyle that the "beautiful people" and their hangers-on held as their private preserve into fare for nimble-footed pre-teens. But the all-out party could not last. The sex, drugs and alcohol took their toll, a backlash set in, and the disco scene faded away.

INDEX